# SINGLE IN AMERICA

BOOKS BY J. L. BARKAS

J. L. Barkas

# SINGLE
# IN
# AMERICA

Atheneum     ⇛*1980*⇚     New York

*All the names used in the material contained in this book have been changed to protect the anonymity of those interviewed.*

Library of Congress Cataloging in Publication Data

Barkas, J. L.
    Single in America.

    Bibliography: p.
    1.  Single people—United States.  I.  Title.
HQ800.B37        305        79-55599
ISBN 0-689-11029-4

Published simultaneously in Canada by McClelland and Stewart Ltd.
Manufactured by American Book–Stratford Press,
Saddle Brook, New Jersey
Designed by Mary Cregan
First Edition

*For Mary Tierney*

# Contents

# SINGLE IN AMERICA

# I

>>>->>>->>>

# Single in America:
# An Overview

I asked a good-looking dentist in his late twenties why he was single. He replied: "Poor people wish they were rich; rich people wish they were happy. Single people wish they were married; and married people wish they were dead." I repeated my question. Hesitantly, he said, "I haven't yet met the perfect woman."

An attractive woman of thirty, who had been divorced for seven years, expressed much the same sentiment, without the initial wariness: "I would get married tomorrow, if I met Mr. Right. I like the whole idea of marriage. The togetherness. The sharing. But I haven't met anyone I wanted who also wanted me." Another young woman related the story of a girlfriend who was desperate to get married: "She wanted to get married in the worst way . . . and did."

How typical are these attitudes toward being single? Who *are* the 56 million single adult men and women in America today? What is singleness really like? Every American adult has to deal with being single; the questions are: when, and for how long? The single years may be those from eighteen until the first marriage, those between a divorce and a second marriage, or those years after the death of a spouse. Singleness may last for the early portion of adulthood, all one's adult years, or as a recurring condition of varying durations.

Very few men and women set out to be single. Instead, many initially search for "the right one," and, unable to find him or her, remain single. Singleness is thrust upon others, following divorce or death of a spouse. Once singleness is perceived to be permanent, a single person wonders, "Why am I single? Is it 'them' or is it 'me'?" This questioning occurs at a different time of life for everyone, although there are some trends. Many bachelors reflect upon their singleness as they near middle age and realize that most of their friends are either married or divorced and that the majority have children. Unmarried women near the age of thirty-five contend with these factors too, but must also deal with an awareness of their biological clock as the safer childbearing years pass by. Singleness tends to be reviewed by the formerly married if, after four or five years of post-divorce singleness, a second marriage has not occurred. Sometimes a reexamination of one's single status is triggered by an event, such as a high school or college reunion (inevitably the question is asked, "Are you married?"), or by a movie (such as *An Unmarried Woman* or *Starting Over*), or by a book (like *I'm Dancing As Fast As I Can*). After holding the first-born infant of a sibling or a close friend, those who want to raise a family will ask themselves: "Why am I still single?"

A man of forty who had never married told me: "One day I sat down and compulsively listed every woman I had dated in the past year. I wrote down why I asked her out, what I didn't like about her, and why I didn't want to see her again." That man reminded me of a woman in her fifties, divorced for ten years, who told me that in just one month she had had over one hundred different dates—for breakfast, lunch, drinks, or dinner. She was searching for Mr. Right. I then thought of a pleasant California man in his mid-thirties who has not married. He lives in a house near San Francisco, sees his girlfriend about four times a week, and teaches cooking at a community college. "Do you think you might someday marry?" I asked. "When I grow in some areas that I have not yet grown in," he replied. "But I gave up searching for the perfect woman. I kept finding her too often. Now I don't have expectations and I don't have disappointments. I just let my relationships happen."

I began to link together all the stories and anecdotes that I had heard over the years from, and about, singles —men and women of all ages who are unmarried, or divorced, or widowed, or living together "without benefit of clergy"—and I recognized certain common characteristics that unite these single men and women, separating them from those who are married. I realized that certain heterosexual or homosexual singles—for instance, those who live together in a relationship—have more in common with married men and women than they do with the unmarried or divorced population.

I discovered that unattached singles who live alone,

in the parental home, or with a same-sex roommate in a platonic relationship, may inhabit a world of often unattainable ideals. Over and over again, these unattached singles would tell me what was wrong with the man or woman they were dating; they were not focused on what was right about that person. By contrast, a happily married woman in her forties compared marriage to adoption. She said: "When you adopt a child, especially an older child with handicaps, you say, 'Well, maybe this isn't the ideal child, but I will grow to love him because I want a child and I want to be a parent. I want the back and forth, the input and the growth, that I will experience and that my spouse will share and that the child will know because I am a parent.' It's similar to when I married. I said to myself, 'My husband has a little bit of this. He doesn't have a little bit of that, but he does have a little bit of this. He's not my ideal, but he has enough of that ideal for me to want to get on with the business of being involved with another person.'"

Most unattached singles, I learned, are still preoccupied with the search. For a multitude of personal and social reasons, which I was determined to understand, they had not yet gotten into "the business of being involved with another person." But why? One factor is that unattached men and women, by associating with other singles, form a cloister of singleness, which allows them to feed on each other's perceptions about romance, relationships, and marriage. I met a divorced woman in her late thirties who admitted that all her close friends of both sexes were currently single, and lived alone. They gathered once a week and, unwittingly, gave reinforcement to each other about the difficulty of forging a mature, loving relationship with someone. "Most of my close friends are single and child-less," a man of thirty told me. "My married sister is de-ciding whether or not she wants to have children. But since most of her close friends are married and parents, she'll probably decide in favor of childbearing."

Over the two years that I researched and wrote this book, I carried out in-depth interviews with two hun-dred singles living in small towns and major cities around the country—in San Francisco, Los Angeles, Sacramento, Laguna Beach, Minneapolis, St. Paul, Chicago, Evanston, Boston, Washington, D.C., Pitts-field, Scranton, Kent, Philadelphia, Ardmore, Madison, Tallahassee, and the greater Metropolitan New York area. I also distributed a six-page questionnaire and received one hundred replies from all types of singles in all sorts of environments, from as far away as Eng-land, India, and Canada.

I spoke with all socioeconomic groups—to a di-vorced woman with three children who is the daughter of one of the wealthiest families in this country, to pro-fessional men and women of all races, to black men and women on welfare, to lower-class whites, to middle-class Hispanics, to middle-class whites, and to those who defy easy classification. Employment status varied widely also—from self-employed businessmen and women, to freelancers, to nine-to-fivers, to those whose work required much travel. I also spoke to dozens of married men and women and, whenever possible, in-terviewed both the husband and the wife. I included as many religious denominations as I could find—Epis-copalians, Universalists, Protestants, Jews, Catholics, Baptists, Jehovah's Witnesses, Hindus, Buddhists, ag-

**7**

nostics, and atheists. I eavesdropped on, and initiated, conversations wherever I happened to be—in cafeterias, restaurants, standing on line for a movie, in theater lobbies, on airplanes, trains, and in taxicabs. All this let me see a variety of situations and meet a wide cross section of men and women. My goal was to identify which traits one-third of the American adult population—those who are single—have in common.

There is a calculated risk in trying to get to the psyche of the single. I did not want to oversimplify or distort a very complex phenomenon. Furthermore, coming to grips with singleness was hampered by the ambivalence and defensiveness of some singles about their state. Initially, they would say: "I'm happy. If someone told me that the rest of my life I would be single, I wouldn't be upset. I enjoy my life. I enjoy my friends. I like my work." But in the next breath they would say: "It's a shallow and empty existence. Living alone is more peaceful, but I miss the emotional intensity and the feedback that comes only from continuing interaction with someone else."

Singles are subject to discrimination. A theater box office may be reluctant, as I discovered, to break up the last pair of seats for a single purchaser. Waiters or waitresses may hurry singles through their meal. Restaurants may make a single patron—especially a single woman—feel uncomfortable, even seating a single at an out-of-the-way table. Singles may be denied the right to purchase a co-op or a house. Employers may feel that singles are "less stable" than their married counterparts, passing them by for promotions or requiring them to relocate or travel more frequently because of a presumed rootlessness. Economic motivation lies behind some, but not all, discrimination. Companies may unintentionally alienate singles by offering invitations to picnics and other outings that suggest "bringing the family." Dinner party hosts or hostesses may be reluctant to invite a single person if it will result in an odd number of guests at the table; and relatives and friends may invade a single's privacy about social matters with questions that they would never dare ask a married person. Some responses singles have developed to "Aren't you married yet?" are: "Not yet. . . . Aren't you divorced by now?" "You'll be the first to know about it." "No." "Depends. Do you fool around?"

I discerned that singles have expectations about marrieds, and marrieds have presumptions about singles, and, in the course of researching this book, I learned that the gulf between singles and marrieds is wider than I had suspected. For example, a divorced woman who visited a married friend at her summer cottage, which she shared with two other couples, told me that she was viewed as a threat, a rival, and an uncomfortable social problem because she was the "odd man out." Rather than as someone with a unique personality, she was prejudged as an aggressive career woman. The unattached single man is, rightly or wrongly, assumed to be having a sexually active social life. A Toronto man who broke up with the woman with whom he had been living for four years suddenly found that his married friends avoided him. "I learned that their wives were afraid that I was bragging about my sexual exploits and that their husbands would begin to stray, accompanying me on these wild escapades." The truth was that he had not had even one date since his relationship terminated two months before. However, the wives

**9**

of his friends may have been right, as some singles do perpetuate the singles myth by bragging about nonexistent exploits because it is expected of them.

I also found that the need to maintain the myths about singleness—that it is a glamorous and fun-filled existence, that it is a time of heightened sexual activity and exotic foreign travels, that it is an enviable state— is great even among former singles; those whom I came to label the "nostalgic single"—the man or woman who, now married and ostensibly content, speaks only with euphoria about his or her unattached and single years. The loneliness and isolation that the majority of unattached singles confess to apparently passed them by, or was, at least, conveniently forgotten.

Singles also have their own views of marriage that may be far from reality, especially if they have never married. "I've had men who have been willing to give me their last names," a single, thirty-five-year-old woman told me, "who have wanted to share a roof with me. But that's not marriage to me. Marriage is a state of mind that most people fail to understand. I don't want to 'be married'; I want the relationship behind the marriage. There were three men with whom I would gladly have gone off into the sunset. But all three made the same mistake. They didn't ask me to marry them." That woman, when she was twenty-five, went to see a psychiatrist who told her: "If you really wanted to be married, you would be." But one cannot simply say, "I don't want to be single anymore." One needs a partner to change singleness.

I did find that there is a prevailing doubt among unattached singles. They wonder, "Do I really want a relationship?" As one woman in her middle-twenties who owns her own printing shop explained, "I don't have time for a relationship. My business comes first. My priorities are to be a success in my business and to make it on my own, without the help of a man." She at least has ordered her priorities, as distinct from those who don't know what they want and consequently have trouble getting it. In talking to those who are married or living together as an alternative to marriage (the "couples type"), I found that the need for a relationship —the emotional and psychological benefits of intimacy— is so widely accepted that to be without someone is anathema. Those unattached singles (the "single type") who, although using different words, still posed the question, "Why join a club that would have me as a member?" appeared to display a lack of the self-love that is a prerequisite to loving someone else.

My investigation led me to read a wide variety of reports, books, papers, articles, and surveys on singleness and marriage. I also interviewed psychologists, lawyers, and social scientists as well as those who counsel or offer services for singles. I took classes on living alone, dealing with separation and divorce, and the legal aspects of marriage. I participated in self-help groups for the widowed, the divorced, and single parents. But the bulk of my findings are based on the probing conversations that I had with the men and women whom I met, interviewed, and reinterviewed over a two-year period. I found that the questions that an enormous number of singles wanted answered were: Are other singles really enjoying life? and Is increasing singleness a healthy trend in our society? This led me to explore the singles industry and how it caters to the inflated numbers of unattached singles and their unmet need for appropriate ways of finding partners. If singles defend their way of life, how many do it because they are really happy being single, and how many do it because it is expected of them? How many because they feel they have no option other than to be unattached and alone? Do unattached singles fear commitment? If they do—and I found that a majority do—how does that fear manifest itself? Is single parenting by choice the ultimate liberation or the ultimate cop-out? But as I interviewed singles the questions that kept coming up were: What is it really like to be a single? Should I want to be single?

In setting out to answer the first of these two questions I soon learned that the quality of one's singleness depends on where one lives, with whom one lives, one's age and sex, whether or not one has primarily single or married friends, and other such variables. But in accordance with what I found to be the key distinguishing traits among singles, I have in this book divided singles into these four categories—*never-marrieds* (those who view their singleness as transitional, those who are unwillingly single, those who are committed to singleness; unwed parents; celibate members of the clergy; homosexuals); *once-marrieds* (separated, divorced, single parents); *widows and widowers;* and *singles in romantic living-together arrangements.*

In arriving at an answer to the second vital question —Should I want to be single?—I had a far harder task. The majority of unattached singles that I interviewed saw their singleness as preferable to living with someone whom they did not love. They would often defend their singleness by saying, "I would have been miserable if I had really married So-and-So" or "How many happily married couples do you know?" In affirming the desirability of singleness by asserting that it is better than enduring a bad relationship, unattached singles deny the existence of a third option—a fulfilling marriage.

When I told singles that my book might be critical of singleness and some of its myths, I met with reluctance from potential interviewees. I soon learned to rephrase my introductory statement, and to point out that I myself am single. I explained that I was "taking an honest look at how singles live." With that less emotive approach I was granted interviews and, ironically, found that the majority of those I interviewed did, indeed, dislike singleness. One woman in her forties, for example, initially refused to fill out my questionnaire or to discuss her singleness. Six months later, however, I called her on quite another matter. "You'll be surprised to know that I'm getting married next month," she exclaimed joyfully. "It all happened six weeks ago." In the next twenty minutes, she gleefully shared how she now viewed her soon-to-be-past single life. "I was fairly content," she noted. "I had a very busy life and I didn't sit around feeling sorry for myself. I could go skiing and play tennis whenever I wanted to. I felt the chances were good that I would be alone for the rest of my life. I had a lot of good friends. But right at dead center, there was a vacuum."

As I researched this book I realized that I was exploring very sensitive issues. I did not, first and foremost, want to misrepresent the single. Fortunately we are past the days of typifying the single as the loser, the misfit, the outcast, the pariah, the fallen woman, the unfeeling man—which is not to say there aren't losers out there. The exaltation of singleness, however, is just as damaging, and as extreme, as the previous clichés that demeaned the single. What I set out to do, when I decided to explore what singleness is all about, was to cut through the extremist views and present, as objectively as possible, singleness as perceived by the singles themselves and, based on my research, how singleness fits into certain larger trends in our society.

There is another fundamental question that I wanted to answer in the course of writing this book: What makes a successful single? There are, certainly, happy and contented singles. I was surprised to learn that, quite often, the most cheerful singles are widows and widowers, regardless of their age. This is not generally true during the period immediately after the death of a spouse, but it is true of the widowed following the resolution of grief—a phase lasting from six months to two years—once they had become resigned to being single or decided actively to seek a new spouse. These "singles by chance" consistently knew what they wanted. They rarely displayed the indecision about whether or not they wanted a lasting relationship that I found in the unmarried single. Nor did they show the bitterness and desperation that I frequently observed in the divorced single. The second group of "happy singles" were those who had chosen living-together relationships as alternatives to marriage who, for most purposes, might just as well be considered married (although the census bureau counts them as single). Whether heterosexual or homosexual, they manifested the "couples-type" personality of marrieds.

The third group of contented singles were the "transitional" singles. These were the single men and women between the ages of eighteen and thirty who could still look ahead optimistically to the possibility of coupling and childbearing. Time would tell whether they simply had not met "the right one" or whether they had an unresolved anxiety about intimacy, for by the age of thirty-five, over 85 percent of Americans are married or have been married. Being single in one's twenties is completely acceptable to the majority of singles. It was rare, I found, to meet disgruntled young "transitional" singles. The diatribes against singleness got louder and harsher from single parents, or after divorce, or with the onset of middle age.

The answer to the question of what makes a satisfied single is of importance not only to singles. It is of vital interest to married people, for there is something that each group can learn from the other. Many married people idealize singleness. It is a fantasy that they need to cling to. Furthermore, as the number of divorced and widowed singles grows, what makes a single contented becomes important no matter what someone's current marital status might be. Americans are becoming more and more aware that singleness, like the common cold, can happen to anyone.

I believe it is no coincidence that the number of singles has grown—increasing 26 percent since 1971 —with the breakdown of the family and the mechanization of life, although the postwar baby boom may also have played a part. Is the rise in singleness a reflection of the glorification of self of the 1970s? Has the unwillingness to "take the good with the bad" led us to lose our staying power in relationships? Does the growth of singleness indicate that long-lasting male-female relationships are considered to be less important than achievements on the job or in other social spheres?

I feel an urgency about these questions because I have discovered that the longer one is single, the easier it is to stay single. Why? Because one develops a single life-style. There is nothing inherently wrong with the world of the unattached single adult, but as the temporary quarters of the single become permanent, so some of the momentum toward coupling is diminished. It is positive for singles to learn to cook for themselves, to be able to eat out alone, to feel comfortable traveling without a companion, but how deep is their independence? Does a relationship bring out their emotional dependency? I discovered that the single unattached adult fears intimacy. The independence that is manifested in living alone or traveling to foreign lands is superficial only. Far more crucial is the way a single relates to his or her partner within an intimate relationship. Is he or she self-reliant or dependent? Does he or she flourish, or does intimacy make that single feel stifled and trapped? "Do you want to rejoin our group this year?" I asked the woman who had shared her imminent wedding plans with me. "I miss our monthly rap sessions," I confided. "To tell you the truth," she answered, "I don't want to be away from Hy for even one night." How does one explain this total turn-around in a woman who has lived alone for most of her adult years?

The biggest hurdle for the majority of unattached singles that I interviewed was learning how to be emotionally self-reliant, and how to blend that self-reliance into a satisfying relationship without becoming overly dependent. Contrary to popular myths about the independent, swinging single, my interviews convinced me that unattached singles are *less* autonomous than those people who are living together or married. Unattached singles have such a strong tendency to be dependent in relationships that, rather than admit to this seeming weakness, they often opt for permanent solitude.

With my research behind me, I am cautious about endorsing the singles phenomenon. For one thing, I believe the never-marrieds who rebelled against their parents in the sixties are going to be settling down into marriage, if only by default: economically, it will be easier for those who marry; two can live almost as cheaply as one, especially in times of continuing inflation when one's standard of living is constantly being eroded.

It is fortunate that singles are not second-class citizens today; that it is finally acceptable to be single is a change for the good. The propagation of anti-marriage views that we have seen in the sixties and seventies, however, is not the way to achieve greater acceptance for unmarried Americans. It is time for a tempered reevaluation of marriage, and in this book, of singleness. There are too many Americans who believe in the clichés about singleness, the hyped-up version of the "swinging single." A twenty-six-year-old accountant I recently met told me, half apologetically and half wistfully, he was getting married the following month. "I really love my fiancée, but somehow I wonder if I'll be missing out on something," he said. "I just finished graduate school and have a well-paying job. I could finally wine and dine a lot of women." Perhaps, had he known about all the consequences of singleness—not just its purported benefits—he would have based his attitude toward marriage on fact, not fancy, and in so doing, made a firmer commitment, whichever path he chose.

# 2

>>>->>>->>>

# The Singles Explosion

Singleness blossomed in American society in the 1970s. The reason for this can be traced to earlier decades: in the late forties, in the aftermath of war, there was an increase in the number of those getting married and starting families. The fifties glorified the family, the housewife with children, and the organization man. The sixties was an era of protest, drug experimentation, and political commitment. The seventies was the decade of self—women of all ages sought economic and professional self-sufficiency as they entered college, graduate school, and the work force in record numbers. Men and women approaching and past middle age reconsidered early career choices and made changes in their home lives and in their jobs as they reassessed life-styles. The singles explosion is real: In the seventies, three sections of the unmarried population sharply increased—those who waited longer to get married; those who divorced and failed to remarry; and those who out-lived their spouses. The total number of single adults eighteen years old and over increased from 43.8 million, in 1971, to 55.8 million, in 1979.

In America today, the 56 million singles—defined as those who are currently not living with a legal spouse —are a varied population:

June has been married and divorced, twice. She now lives with her ten-year-old daughter.

Bob, a middle-aged engineer, will continue living alone until the "right one comes along."

Judy, a college senior, has her own apartment about a mile from campus. She doesn't plan to marry until she has established herself in her career.

Steve, a lawyer in his mid-thirties, does not have a very active social life; he lives alone and for his career. He is gay.

Marion is in her late twenties and has never married. She and her five-year-old daughter live in a two-family home in North Philadelphia. Marion has a full-time job, attends college, and also receives public assistance.

Sal is an elderly widower. Since his wife died a few years ago, he has lived with his married children. But he would like to remarry.

George is from Cleveland; Mildred is from Sioux City. They met in college and have lived together in an eastern city for the last fifteen years.

Joan is twenty-five years old and has always lived with her parents. She expected to be married by now, but things didn't work out that way for her.

Mark has two children. He has been divorced for the last three years; he shares a two-bedroom apartment with another divorced man. Mark sees his children on weekends.

Sally, who is thirty-one, has two small children. Her husband was killed five years ago by a robber.

Nina dresses fashionably and smokes cigarettes. She is forty-one, teaches, has never married and probably never will. She has been a nun for the past twenty years.

Sara is a physician in her late thirties. She is divorced and lives and works in Denver. She has not had sex in two years.

This sampling goes some way to illustrate the range of age, background, and living arrangements of single adults, who now inhabit one out of every five households in this country. The census bureau predicts that singleness will continue to increase; by 1990, it is projected that one out of every four households will contain a single adult.

Not all singles live alone. Indeed, of the 56 million single adults in America today, more than two thirds do not live alone. They live with a friend, lover, or relative. Warren, for example, is a real estate broker who has been engaged four times. He owns a home on Long Island and has two roommates—one male and one female—who pay him for rent and for food. Linda and Joyce live together in a renovated brownstone; they are both divorced and alternate caring for their children so that each one can work part-time.

One of the myths about singleness is that it is accepted as a permanent state primarily by upper-income career men and women in their late thirties and forties. Yet people at all economic levels are now considering conventional marriage as just one of several options, and prolonging their singleness, at least temporarily. A black man who earns $5,000 a year told me: "I'm only twenty-seven. That's too young to be thinking about marriage. Besides, when I marry, I'm going to marry a woman who will improve my situation. I don't want to marry someone who's going to be a drain on me. Right now my car is my wife."

Confusion and uncertainty often tinge the social world of the single. If someone becomes single at forty, having last been single twenty years before, he or she tends to be unpracticed at current dating etiquette. A friend of mine, who is a journalist and a single parent, explained that her ex-husband is very reluctant to ask a woman out on a date. "When he does go out, it's usually because someone has invited him to do something. He waits for that." Most men in similar situations find that except for an infrequent phone call from a woman, the old rules still stand—the man is the one to call and the one to pay. Exceptions and variations to the old rules are more numerous now, however. Women have been known to sue for breach of promise, but the tables were recently turned when a California accountant sued his date for $38 in expenses, because she stood him up. One wonders how quickly she accepted another date. One also wonders how quickly he did.

Singles are given conflicting messages: learn to enjoy the life of a single, learn to live alone without being lonely, and learn to give up the idea that one needs to love and be loved, but at the same time, learn how to share, how to meet people, how to love, and how to become an integral part of a couple. Advice to singles is often dogmatic. One book, for example, offers, "I'm single, and I'm happy. You can be happy this way too. Read on." Another gives advice in "loneliness tolerance training"—"guidelines for programming and getting control of the time you spend alone." Yet another popular work, intended for the over-fifty single, explains: "As time went on, the rewards and compensation of single living accumulated for these people, as they can for you, if you are willing to make the effort to re-establish joy in your life."

To some, being single is as intrinsic to their way of life as being coupled is to their married counterparts. To others, being single is a temporary condition until the right person comes along. Singleness can thus be viewed as either a permanent or a transitional state. Whether singleness is transitional or permanent is more a function of how the individual views his or her situation than of the duration of that state. Some of those who are committed to singleness describe their feelings with missionary zeal—"I think everyone should be single," says a physician in his early forties. "Who needs the headaches of marriage?" Or, as an elderly widow explains, "I have my friends. I have my children. I have enough money. Why should I need another man?" But even unwilling singles—those who bemoan their inability to find a satisfactory partner—are sensitive about the right of the single to be unmarried. "Our culture places such a premium on marriage," a single woman in her thirties told me, "and I don't think that's right. But I don't think singleness is the glamorous life that people have been led to think it is." That woman expressed to me fear of the responsibility that marriage entailed; she did not have plants in her apartment, she explained, because she was reluctant to have to devote consistent care to anything.

Unmarried men and women gave these three primary reasons for remaining single: *commitment to career, independence,* and *not having met the right one.* These were the words, and phrases, that men and women used to describe the reasons for and benefits of their single status:

"self-reliance"

"privacy"

"freedom to do whatever I feel like doing without the responsibility to a partner"

"at this point, the most important thing to me is my career"

"can't find the right girl"

"have not met *her!*"

"the guys I want to marry don't want to marry me, but the ones who want to marry me, I don't want to marry"

"I'm not psychologically ready yet"

"I don't think I want to have a family"

"can't afford it"

"enjoy the chase too much"

"married men get so boring"

"a strong sense of territory and self"

"complete independence"

"not having to clean my place spotlessly clean all the time"

"sleeping better"

"better concentration at home"

"planning my existence is simplified"

"solitude"

"freedom of movement, choice, and of life-style"

Although both committed and transitional singles pointed out drawbacks to being single, they saw these as manageable and not outweighing the benefits of singleness. Unwilling singles—who were "single by default"—could not see many positive features in their state. As one unmarried forty-year-old professor noted, "I find being single too painful even to think about it. There are no advantages to it." The most frequent complaints about being single were *loneliness* or *lack of companionship* and (from men) *unfamiliarity with performing household chores*. Typical descriptions of the disadvantages of being single included:

**25**

"lack of someone to share with"

"trouble lining up a date"

"no one to care for me when I'm sick"

"loneliness"

"I tend to feel neglected"

"it's depressing at times"

"sometimes you want company and you don't want to impose on your female friends, who are deeply involved with their men" (woman)

"waking up in the morning"

"cleaning, washing, and shopping" (man)

"how do you fold fitted sheets?" (man)

"I get lonely"

"the weekends stink"

"sexual dissatisfaction"

"no one to talk to or listen to at the end of the day"

"no one to kill the bugs" (woman)

"I hate eating alone"

"gin rummy beats the hell out of solitaire"

Must a number of years pass before a single person accepts his or her status and stops searching for a spouse? I found that there are trends: the women who told me they had "given up hope" were in their mid to late thirties; the men who told me they were not the "marrying kind" were in their early forties, or had come to that decison at that age. In *Passages,* Gail Sheehy notes that for the widow or widower, singleness can be "good," a period of self-discovery and growth, "especially if one's light has been eclipsed by a mate's dominant personality. . . ." But for the unmarried male nearing his fourth decade, or female approaching thirty, singleness is often seen as a "crisis," with subsequent panic reactions. It seems ironic to panic at not being part of an institution from which one may desperately wish liberation some years later.

Other philosophers on the singles condition make pronouncements about whether singleness is "good" or "bad." In *Lonely in America,* Suzanne Gordon is resentful that many singles wish to be otherwise. She notes in her chapter on singlehood that "most single people still believe in the myth of the one, despite all the current evidence of the instability of such exclusive bonds. They also believe that the lack of the 'one' is the primary cause of their loneliness. . . . A solitary person must, by definition, be lonely. . . . But how not be lonely in a society that places you in exile because you do not have a mate? . . . We are a 'couple culture.' "

Is the "couple culture" a major reason some singles wish to be otherwise? For some, singleness is not a viable alternative to marriage. Joanna Kyd, a theater critic and advertising copywriter, summed up her disenchantment with singleness in an article titled "Unmarriage." Kyd, who had just separated from her husband, describes the various stages she went through in adjusting to post-marriage realities. She has a date with someone who puts down marriage by explaining, " 'All

I know is I couldn't afford all the therapy it takes to stay married.'" But Kyd is not convinced that being single is all that attractive either. "I'll never forget how lost those souls seemed," she concludes. "How lost I felt. These are real unmarried people. Marriages don't seem to work any more, but there's a new lost generation that grows bigger every day. Because the truth is that unmarriage doesn't work either."

For some, however, singleness *is* better than marriage. "I realized that I didn't want to have children," a Minnesota man told me. "I come from a family of eight and I have enough nephews and nieces to keep me busy. I like my independence. I live with a woman if it seems right, or I live alone and have my friends. I'm never lonely. I don't want the responsibility of a wife and family." A thirty-seven-year-old divorced Chicago woman told me: "I'm single because I was unhappy with the man I was married to. I didn't want to wake up at fifty and wonder why I hadn't gotten out of the marriage twenty years earlier. I'm terrified of making another mistake; I don't want to be one of those women who marries three or four times."

In spite of the increase in the number of single adults in America today, national public opinion polls indicate that marriage, rather than singleness, is the preferred state. The 1980 Virginia Slims Poll found that 96 percent of 3,000 women and 1,000 men interviewed preferred marriage as a way of life. Only 2 percent of the women and 1 percent of the men chose remaining single and living alone as "best as a way of life." Considering that one out of every two or three marriages in America today ends in divorce, and that widows outnumber widowers by five to one, the expressed public preference for marriage may be more idealistic than realistic. Indeed, in 1979, 39.5 percent of women over eighteen and 32.9 percent of men over the age of eighteen were single. As is so often true, people say one thing and do the opposite.

Although most singles are still concentrated in urban areas, an increasing number are settling in suburban and rural communities. As the cost of living increases, singles are often forced to live with same-sex room-mates to save on rent. The geographic clustering of singles is a conseqeunce of their minority status, as well as of economics. Like other minorities, singles tend to search out and champion their own. Although there are exceptions, singles are generally more com-fortable with other singles. They differ significantly from married people in their concerns and in their ori-entations. Contented marrieds reported that the eve-nings and the weekends were the cherished parts of their week—the time to be with spouse and family; the unattached singles who were not actively dating said just the opposite—that after work and on weekends they were most acutely aware of their loneliness. As one divorced woman in her early thirties explained: "The weekends are so bad that I actually look forward to work on Monday."

Although the largest component of singles is the 10½ million widows and the 2 million widowers (who tend to be elderly), it is the unmarried men and women in their twenties and thirties that come to mind when someone says "singles." Indeed, there have been in-creases in the percentages of men and women in that age group who are remaining single. From 1960 to 1978, the percentage of the population remaining single in the eighteen- to twenty-four-year-old group increased by 43 percent (for men) and 40 percent (for women). In the twenty-five- to twenty-nine-year-old age group, the percentage increases were from 21 to 22 percent (for men) and 10 to 14 percent (for women). Combine this with the percentage increase of twenty-to-thirty-year-olds with respect to the general population, as well as the absolute increase in population, and large numbers of singles appear.

Do these statistics represent rejection of marriage and the family atmosphere in which these men and women matured? Not inconsistently, this group, raised during a period when material wealth was emphasized and the nuclear family was disintegrating, has opted for a way of life that is dependent on an extended family of peers, rather than on a more restricted one-to-one relationship. There has been so much emphasis in the post–World War II American culture on material success at any price that the value of family and love has been minimized. Rather than seeing life as a composite of relationships and achievements, only the tangible measures of success were considered. As instant foods replaced home cooking, so instant relationships have rivaled marriage, and divorce is the ready answer when marriage founders. Dishwasher broken? Throw it out and buy another one. Discontent with a romantic relationship or a marriage? Break it off rather than try to repair it. And yet a married woman in Wisconsin told me that she might have published five books in her forty years, instead of two, had she not had the extra burdens of holding down a part-time job and raising three adolescents. But, she confessed, she would not trade her husband or her children for the accomplishments of a single woman half her age who had managed to publish ten books.

Often singles are extremely concerned with the material benefits their presumptive spouse will add to their lives. A divorced woman in her early thirties explained, "If I got married again, it would be so that I would never have to work. My prince charming is going to make at least one hundred thousand a year or I'm just not going to be interested." The only reason some see for marriage is the betterment of their material status. "I'm not particularly fond of the man that I'm dating," a single woman in her late twenties told me, "but he takes me to the ballet and likes to go to nice expensive restaurants. He might just turn out to be a good 'catch.'"

The singles explosion of the 1970s was also tied to the increase in the number of young men and women who moved out of their parents' homes before they were emotionally ready. After a time, feelings of desperation and discontent at unfulfilled expectations set in, and some of these singles would make unfortunate choices in relationships, marry quickly, and eventually divorce. Others would alternate periods of living alone and living with a romantic partner. Or they would move back home, often after some years of post-school singleness, to settle into a permanently single and dependent life.

With one third of all Americans now single, it is not surprising that a singles industry has emerged—to the tune of over $40 billion a year. It is an industry concerned with making money. There are local and national clubs and activities geared to singles only, singles bars, singles apartment complexes, singles dating services, and singles vacations. Even those who have been raised in more traditional, family-oriented settings are influenced by media and business glorification of self, guiding them away from old-fashioned love, marriage, and family. "Should I really care about her the way I do?" asks one twenty-three-year-old single man. "Everyone out there is telling me that I shouldn't be content with a normal, healthy, loving relationship with one woman. That I should want this swinging single life. Maybe there's something wrong with me?" Maybe there's something wrong with them.

Although there are other ways to seek a partner besides the singles bars, singles housing complexes, and computer-dating organizations, it takes more exploring, planning, initiative, and imagination to find out what and where they are. Many singles are too embarrassed, reluctant, or lazy to search for them. Plugging into a computer-dating service may require only one fee and one application. Placing an ad in the local newspaper necessitates composing the announcement, contacting the publication, paying for one or more notices, and screening the applicants. Although introductions to potential partners by friends and associates, I learned, are excellent ways of meeting new people, someone first has to make the offer. There is still some stigma attached to being "fixed up," and out of pride, many singles will not ask their friends if they know anyone interesting. At the same time, their friends may not offer for fear of giving offense.

There has been a proliferation of literature on singleness. One reviewer commented on the bulging number of books aimed at singles and concluded: "Families and couples step aside. It is now apparently time for singles to be exploited." True enough. An avalanche of pro-single books appeared in the 1970s: *Single Blessedness; First Person Singular; How to Be Single Creatively; Single: Living Your Own Way; For Singles Only; The Whole Single Person's Catalog; Lifelines: Learning to Live Alone Without Being Lonely; Single After 50: How to Have the Time of Your Life; Living Single Successfully; Flying Solo; The Challenge of Being Single; The Single Parent Experience; Single; Single Women, Alone and Together; MOMMA: The Sourcebook for Single Mothers;* and on and on.

The mass media also discovered the singles explosion. In 1978 and 1979 alone, New York's *WomensWeek,* a metropolitan newspaper for women, devoted an entire issue to "Being Single"; playwright and novelist Bruce Jay Friedman published *The Lonely Guy's Book of Life; Self,* a national magazine, appeared at the beginning of 1979, filled with articles on loneliness, "single and dating again," living together, and so on. Dozens of other major features appeared on a regional and national basis, such as "Going It Alone" in *Newsweek;* "Unmarried Life Style" and "Manhattan Singles" in *Cue;* "Teaching Poetry Writing to Singles" in the *New Yorker;* and "Goodbye to Marriage" in the *New York Review of Books.* Each day during the week of April 14, 1979, the New York Telephone Company offered Dr. Joyce Brothers with "a different message on how to make the single life the good life," as the ad in the *New York Times* put it. The advertising world, too, has learned how to appeal to that part of the single community that wants to find a partner; all it need do is convey the notion that a product or a service will increase sex appeal, or, sharpening focus, help in finding a mate.

A booming part of the singles industry is the surge of health and sports clubs that cater—often at exorbitant cost—to the unmarried trade. Attractiveness is a vital concern of the single person—studies in the United States, Canada, Germany, and Japan have shown that people tend to be attracted to those who are as attractive as they are—and in addition to the health benefits of shaping up and staying fit there is the expectation that new relationships will evolve out of the club experience. Paradoxically, however, although the majority of people who exercise at clubs after work are single, there is very little communication between strangers. Getting in shape is the all-important thing. The singles culture is so physique conscious that older and out-of-shape singles are at a decided disadvantage if they wish to have an active social life. A single man who attended a singles weekend in the mountains told me: "I was amazed at how these obese women had the nerve even to come. They showed up at the disco and they actually expected some guy to ask them to dance. But all the men were interested in the good-looking ones." This from a man who was himself no prize on the surface. Women that I interviewed resented the stress on appearances that is part and parcel of the singles world. But the rules are there if one wants to play the dating/mating game. A single woman in her thirties recently told me that since she has separated from her husband, she is far more concerned with her weight than she was when she was married. She always cared about her looks, she added, but it had now become a matter of life and death to her. The overemphasis on the external frightened her. She thought she was beyond that. "It seems so high school," she complained.

The singles industry is far more than just swimming pools, tennis clubs, skiing weekends, and chartered flights abroad. In the Bay Area of San Francisco, where singles outnumber marrieds, there are some fifty groups for singles, including clubs for booklovers, intellectuals, and epicureans. In New York City, there are more than thirty established organizations that cater to singles. One organization even publishes a directory and activity list of those clubs. The range of the singles organizations is vast—from purely social ones, such as cocktail, dinner, and disco parties, dances and coffee hours, to cultural events such as theater parties, concerts, discussion groups and seminars. Singles are also organized around social service themes, such as volunteering to aid the handicapped, providing reading and activity programs for children in shelters, and participating in civic projects for orphans and underprivileged youngsters. (For several years, I belonged to one of New York City's largest sports clubs—35,000 members; 12,000 singles. Through it I became active in a women's volunteer group started by another member. For two years, we aided female offenders, first in the state penitentiary, and then after their release.)

If you were alone last New Year's Eve, for an admission fee you could have met "hundreds of singles" at the parties sponsored by "singles only" clubs. Singles "hot lines," parallelling those of such other groups as potential suicides, gays, and runaways, have also been established. If one night in April 1980 you had called a 24-hour recording service with daily singles activities in New York, you would have been informed of a chamber music concert, a mixer at a church, a Jewish religious service, a lecture by a psychologist, and a private champagne party.

There are national groups of singles, such as Parents Without Partners, based in Washington, D.C.; Divorce Anonymous, headquartered in Chicago; America's Society of Divorced Men, in Elgin, Illinois; the Displaced Homemakers Network, in Baltimore; the National Association for Divorced Women, in New York City; or the National Association of Christian Singles, in Kansas City. At the local level, there are self-help support groups for singles, widows, divorced persons, gays, single parents, and live-ins. In addition to private counseling services, there are low-cost ones attached to mental health clinics, hospitals, graduate psychology programs, and nonsectarian charitable organizations. Groups, led by therapists, social workers, or peers, meet in synagogues, churches, and branches of the YMCA or YWCA. College and adult education programs offer courses in "how to be single," "how to deal with loneliness," "how to be your own best friend," "how to meet people," and "how to achieve autonomy." In 1978, there was a Singles Expo organized at a hotel in Los Angeles; 1,200 singles attended workshops and seminars. The following year, a three-day conference, "On Being Single," was held at Fallen Leaf Lake, California.

Most singles groups that flourish are those that have meeting a mate as a secondary enticement, the primary one being shared interests. I observed a two-hour weekly arts and crafts group for widows and widowers over the age of sixty-five; friendship was an outgrowth of their mutual need to keep busy in a creative way. One weekend, I joined 250 men and women between the ages of twenty and forty—70 percent were single— for two and a half days at a summer camp for adults that is located in Kent, Connecticut. For an all-inclusive price, meals, activities, and lodging—four in a cabin— were provided; round-trip bus fare from Manhattan was available for a minimal charge. Unlike singles bars— which offer little more than drinks, a place, and conversation that is geared toward being "picked up"— this camp provided a wide range of individual and group activities—horseback riding, roller disco, exercise classes, swimming, waterskiing, hiking, canoeing, mini-marathon runs, and entertainers in the evenings. One twenty-five-year-old, however, whose roommate characterized her as "desperate" about her singleness, left after only one day; she said she felt uncomfortable in the co-ed setting. Of course many phone numbers were exchanged and, according to the owners, "many" couples who met there are now married or living together.

I met one man in his early forties, who had never been married, who organized a lecture series, on themes ranging from city architecture to food and nutrition. For each event he charged four dollars per person for the first two years and five dollars the third year. Over the three-year period, ten thousand singles participated in his social gatherings. "If you met someone," he explains, "it was a side benefit." Did the group improve his own social life? "I dated about fifty women that I met through my organization," he confessed, "but nothing ever 'clicked.'" Another man I met, who is now married and in his late twenties, remembers as a child the meetings for single parents that his newly divorced father took him to. "I knew we were there mainly so my Dad could meet women who were in his situation," he explains. Another woman that I interviewed advertised in a local newspaper and gave weekly parties for singles for a fee. Over a two-year period, she had forty parties, with twelve to fifteen participants each. The parties had themes (discussion of the latest Woody Allen movie) or provided a performer, such as a hypnotist, guitar player, or horoscope reader. Although she met only two men whom she saw again socially, she enjoyed the Saturday night events. It was a way to meet new people, make a small profit, and avoid wondering what she would do on "date night."

There are some sound economic reasons for the business community's concern about the single population. Single men and women, who have been increasingly represented in the labor force, have growing disposable income. In 1977, for example, singles in the eighteen- to forty-year-old age bracket took three times as many vacations as their married contemporaries; singles bought 17 percent of the homes and 25 percent of all new cars.

The full-time single worker without children has a spending pattern similar to that of an adolescent, in that he or she tends to buy nonessential goods for personal enjoyment and to enhance his or her status. Once singles pay for basic living costs—rent or mortgage payments, transportation, clothing, and food—their salaries can be used for entertainment, travel, accoutrements, and extravagances—discretionary income. Many married couples with families are happy to eat out once a week; many singles may dine at home only once a week.

Salaries for women—married or single—are generally $4,000 to $8,000 lower than they are for men in comparable jobs, so the single woman has a harder time financially than the single man. The extra monetary demands of socializing, including taxicabs home late at night or the purchase of a car, may be out of reach for some single women in lower-income jobs, and they must depend on regular or intermittent male escorts to "take them out" if they wish to socialize at all. The single to suffer the most severe economic pressure is the single mother. Half of all the families run by single mothers were below the poverty level in 1977. Yet only 9 percent of the families with breadwinning fathers were as poor. Few single mothers are as fortunate as one woman, a TV commercial producer, whose company provides her with a full-time housekeeper for her infant. Most find it so difficult to meet their bills, and pay for child care, that they must resort to second or third jobs. I met a single parent with two adolescents whose income was so low one year that the government complimented her resourcefulness by auditing her; it looked suspicious that she had managed to survive on such meager funds. Another single mother found that moving back to her parents' home, and going on welfare until her baby was old enough to start school, was the only solution to her financial predicament. Another divorced mother has had to give her three-year-old daughter to her mother, who lives in another state, to raise, so that she can finish a training program that will provide her with employable skills.

What are the psychological and physical consequences if "the right one" never does come along? There are some startling statistics about the higher incidence of disease, hospital admissions and suicide for singles, as compared to a comparable group of marrieds. My own research qualified those findings, in that there are distinctive factors that exaggerate or minimize the effects of singleness: job satisfaction, proximity of nuclear family, mixture of married and single friends, hobbies or activities outside of work, economic status, residential circumstances, and whether or not someone was "dating," regardless of the outcome of such socializing. As one single woman of twenty-eight, who likes her job, her friends, and her apartment, told me: "As long as I have a steady boyfriend, I don't consider myself single. It's the period between men that's hardest to get through. But I don't know if I'll feel the same way about living alone in another ten years."

Is the choice of singleness or marriage a matter of luck? A New York cab driver had his own view. Reaching to the glove compartment for pictures of his children and their families, he said: "That's my daughter-in-law. She was just lucky that she found my son. He has only one God and one woman. And here's my daughter. She's been married twelve years, and are they happy. Me, I met my wife in Russia and the next day, we got married, for three rubles. It's luck. It's like driving a cab. Some days I'll drive around without any business. Or then I'll catch a fare going to Kennedy Airport and another coming back into the city. Driving a cab and marriage. It's luck, I tell you."

His view may be sound, but this book will focus on factors we can hope to control and understand. There is a part of all of us that still believes in "Once upon a time . . . and they lived happily ever after," but we all want something better than a fairy tale. We want to start creating our own luck.

# 3

-≫-≫-≫

## Single by Choice?—
## The Never-married

Despite the singles explosion, over 90 percent of Americans are married by the age of thirty-five; those who never marry are a gaining, but still small, minority. This chapter deals with those American men and women, over the age of eighteen, who are not married and never have been. Except for celibate members of religious orders, and those who are presently cohabiting, most of these singles, I discovered, are still seeking a partner. The vast majority of them are "transitional" singles, for whom singleness is a hallway, not a destination. Transitional singles want to find a mate. They attempt to make the most of their singleness, but accept their eventual coupling and, generally, parenting as a natural progression.

For a small number of men and women, singleness is seen as, and thus becomes, a permanent state—an alternative to marriage. These permanent, committed singles are content to be unattached. They find satisfaction in their family, friends, work, hobbies, outside interests, and romantic liaisons.

There is one last group of unmarried men and women: those who wished their singleness had been transitional but found that it became permanent. These "unwilling" singles are disgruntled and outspoken against singleness. These are the ones who implore, "Where are the decent men?" or "Why can't I find a woman?" I discovered a distinct pattern to their attitudes toward relationships. These never-marrieds are naïve and almost childlike in their unwillingness to settle for anyone less than the "perfect" spouse. They tend to apply the same standards to themselves that they apply to potential mates and are, as a group, overly critical and driven. They see intimacy as a condition that will cost them rather than benefit them.

It is well worth taking a closer look at the majority of never-married men and women today—those who are prolonging their singleness by postponing the time when they marry. These transitional singles might be called "single today, married whenever." My own research indicates that what we are seeing in this population is a return to a later marrying age rather than a permanent rejection of wedlock.

Why is marriage being postponed in America today? I observed that the following factors account for the growth of singleness: financial limitations, prolonged education, career commitment, increased acceptability of singleness, fear of making a mistake (divorce), delay of childbearing and parenting responsibility, legalization of abortion, contraceptives ("safe sex"), and acceptability of living alone outside the parental home (women, primarily).

Economic pressures today, as well as the practical need for advanced education, have necessitated the postponement of marriage—and led to an increase in post-school singlenesses. The necessity of college and even graduate education has led to an extended adolescent and dependent phase for many young Americans. (At the turn of the century, only about 20 percent of the population went on to college; the rest were working or married. Today, those figures are reversed; trade schools, junior colleges, colleges, universities, or graduate schools are virtual necessities in the quest for career and material success.) On college campuses today, seniors talk about moving to their first apartment, and with whom they will live, with the same fervor that ten years ago was accorded to marital engagements.

Some adults *never* feel that their income could include the financial dependence of another person, or children. "Why haven't I married?" a thirty-year-old salesman who lives in New Jersey asked rhetorically. "Because I can't afford to. I can just about pay my rent and keep up my car payments. I don't know if I'll ever be able to afford a wife." It used to be that only men would say that they wished to establish themselves in their careers, achieve a good income, and travel before settling down. A growing number of women, either seeking careers of their own or accepting that divorce or death might thrust them into a self-supporting or child-supporting role, are opting for a "life before marriage." Indeed, nearly three times as many women were enrolled in college in 1970 as in 1960, an increase from 1.2 million to 3 million women (to 4.8 million in 1977). As women pursue more education, and more challenging jobs, fewer of them are willing to put their husbands through college or graduate school by taking on low-level work. Since young men are struggling to complete their own education and get established in a career, fewer of them are willing to make the sacrifices called for in marrying a young female student who has current high educational costs and no immediate earning capacity.

Susan, a twenty-year-old black woman from Harrisburg, Pennsylvania, does not intend to marry until she is at least twenty-five. During the school year, she lives in the dormitory of an urban university. Susan has a straight A average and plans to go on to law school. "I've gone steady with guys while I'm in school," Susan told me, "but it's hard on them because they can't accept how much time I put into my books. I set my priorities with my books. I study at least five hours a night and most of the weekend. Sometimes I get lonely. But when I'm home, there are one or two men whom I can call up, go out with, have a nice time with, and if I want to have sex, that's fine too. I haven't found anyone here at school with whom I can have a similar 'no strings attached' relationship." Marilyn, who is thirty, is finishing her Ph.D. in psychology at a university in Minnesota. She expresses a view similar to Susan's: "It's been in the back of my mind that I didn't want to get involved with anyone until I got the degree finished. In six months, when I finally get it, I'll be more open to marriage."

The delaying of first marriage is an outgrowth of the

**45**

far-reaching women's liberation movement. Staying home and raising a family is now considered one alternative of several. It will take a reversal of the trend in social thought to see a return to the glorification of the full-time housewife of the 1950s. Inflation and the ever-increasing endorsement by men of wage-earning wives testifies that working women—and working mothers—are becoming the rule, rather than the exception. Indeed, nearly 50 percent of all married women in 1979 worked compared to only 15 percent in 1940. There are still, however, some jobs that are commoner to men than to women, and women who want to enter certain male-dominated fields often find they must—temporarily at least—choose singleness. At one company, for example, where extensive traveling is required, fourteen out of sixteen salesmen are married, but all three of the saleswomen are single. Prejudices against women are still common. It will be some time before men—or employers—are as accepting of demanding careers for women as wives have been for centuries with regard to their husbands' careers.

I discovered that the majority of young unmarried men and women feel that the pressure to marry comes from within, rather than from peers or from parents. "Most of my married friends are always telling me how lucky I am to be single," a statistician in his early twenties told me. "When I was thinking of getting married (in one of my less lucid moods) they were the ones who persuaded me to wait." He is dating a girl whom he met through a friend two years ago. The relationship has been temporarily "shelved" since he moved to another city to take a job with a big firm. What would make being single easier for him? "Being single is already too easy," he replied. A twenty-four-year-old graduate student, who had just broken up with her fiancé, with whom she had been living for two years, told me: "I felt stigmatized when I was living with my boyfriend because most of my friends are single and they viewed me as married." A handsome man of twenty-eight, who is working as a waiter while he tries to make it as an actor, expressed a similar view. "I don't feel pressure from anybody else to get married," he told me, "only from myself. Most of my friends are single. I don't think so much about being married as I do about doing things with someone who would be like a spouse. My ideal single state would be seeing someone on weekends."

Ironically, the single men and women who told me their parents were keenly in favor of marriage post-ponement—"What's your rush?"—"Get yourself a firm financial base first"—are not always products of un-happy marriages. It is the parent who has had a rela-tively happy marriage, but feels that his or her career ambitions were thwarted by early marriage, who stresses "career first, marriage later" to a child. Because marriage often lessens dependence on the nuclear fam-ily, it is also possible that this parental emphasis on career and singleness is a way in which parents try to hold on to their offspring.

Regardless of age, most of the unmarried women who told me that their mothers discouraged them from marrying were not only career oriented; they were bent on fame. "I have some need for accomplishment, for making a mark on the world beyond taking care of a husband and children," a woman in her mid-thirties told me. "That's why I'm not looking for a man right now." Of all the single women that I spoke to, these were the saddest. Some were so bent on recognition that they ceased dating in their early twenties and worked around-the-clock at their vocations. Barbara, who is thirty-one and works as a waitress to support herself as she tries to make it as an actress, grew up in a middle-class home. Her mother was a nonworking housewife who complained daily about the meaninglessness of her life and how she wished she had never married and had instead pursued a career. Barbara and her younger brother, who is also unmarried, rarely heard a kind word about their father, or marriage, from their mother. Barbara's mother is still married, after thirty-five years, but Barbara is unable to sort out the contradiction between the messages she heard as a child and her mother's current emphasis on "So when are you getting married already?" Mildred, a writer in her thirties, has recently been reevaluating her decision to focus all her energies on building a literary reputation at the price of her social life. But she fails to see how her mother's constant criticisms of marriage and homemaking are a possible source of her own unmarried and career-oriented life-style. "When are you getting married?" her mother asks in their long-distance phone calls; the same mother who bemoaned bearing ten children and failing to have a career of her own. Paul, a musician in his early thirties, has never been involved with a woman for longer than a year. At times he wonders if his fear of marriage is related to his father's belief that family obligations prevented him from becoming the performer he thought he could have been. "Marriage and raising a family is hard," a thirty-year-old single man is constantly reminded by his father, who drives a taxi—the same father who also says, "So when are you getting married?"

Single men and women, whether living at home or living alone, are more available to their parents than if they married. "I go over to my parents on Saturday night if I don't have a date," a physician in his late twenties told me. "I don't like to go out alone. Why shouldn't I spend that time with my parents if I have the night free? I also see them every Sunday, and if nothing much is happening in my social life, I stop by several times a week. Now my sister, who's living with a graduate student, doesn't see them that often. Her boyfriend and my father don't get along. It has hurt my father a great deal that she has cut herself off from him."

Over and over again, never-married singles of all ages gave the establishment and advancement of a career as their first goal; finding the right marriage partner as their second. But there is a vicious cycle at work here; the steadfast pursuit of a career has meant that these singles leave themselves less ready opportunity to meet "the right one." Many will work late and go directly home from the office. "I can't wait to get home, have dinner, and get a good night's sleep," a twenty-nine-year-old unmarried man who has a middle-management job told me. He restricts his social life to Saturday night, if he was lucky enough to chance upon a potential date sometime during the previous week. At work, career-oriented single men and women are concerned with their performance and not with hunting for possible mates. At home, they settle down to eating a meal, working, relaxing with television, making phone calls, and seem unwilling, or unable, to go out and "look." Of all the never-married singles that I interviewed, only a few told me that they had met someone at their job or in transit to and from their home and office. One woman became involved with the exterminator and locksmith who serviced her apartment building "and then serviced me," as she put it. Another woman was asked out by an ophthalmologist who lived in her building, whom she had first seen in the elevator. But generally, after the school years, it takes effort rather than "dumb luck" to find a suitable partner.

Richard Yates, a senior staff psychologist at the University of Iowa student counseling service, has seen an increase in skepticism about marriage in his client population—men and women from the ages of eighteen to twenty-six. "I'm hearing a lot more anti-marriage talk than I did, say, ten years ago," Yates says. "They say to me, 'Why get married? So many people are unhappy and they end up getting divorced anyway.'" High divorce statistics—40 percent of the number of marriages last year—are evidence of that disillusionment.

As the advantages of having children are weighed against the emotional and financial toll, many men and women postpone marriage because they also want to postpone—and possibly avoid—childbearing. In 1971, when females born during the baby boom of the 1940s entered their childbearing years and the birthrate was expected to have increased, a decrease was noted. The fertility rate reached an all-time low in American history in 1976 and has not risen significantly yet. Most men and women still associate marriage with parenting. "If I do get married, I would do it only because I want to have children" was the familiar refrain that I heard, on this occasion from an eighteen-year-old college freshman. "It used to be that you married to have sex," an older woman told me, "but now you can have that outside marriage, so wanting a family has become the main motivation for marriage."

The legalization of abortion and its increased social acceptance, combined with the widespread availability of contraceptives, has minimized the "shot-gun marriage" syndrome. There are certainly hundreds of thousands of single parents—by choice and by accident—but any number of women and men who might, ten years ago, have "had" to marry have been able to remain single. One woman, who married at the age of thirty, is grateful that she had two abortions during her twenties and that she did not marry either man. "I was so mixed up," she explains, "neither situation would have lasted." She now has one child by her husband and is trying to get pregnant again. "I had an abortion when I was twenty-six," an older single woman told me. "At that time, it was a scandalous act. But I didn't want to get married—and still don't. I never even told the father, because I knew the marriage wouldn't have worked. I don't feel guilty. It was the right thing to do."

The growth of transitional singleness has also been aided by the social trends that have sanctioned single women living in their own apartments or homes. As recently as the 1940s, most young women did not live outside the parental home unless it was with a husband. Now, not only has it become acceptable for a woman to live alone (if she can afford it), or with another female, but she can even have a male roommate without too many tongues wagging.

Is it advisable to delay making a long-term emotional commitment until the end of one's twenties, or even well into the thirties? For some, there is no choice.

Others simply do not come into their own until their thirties, and for them, the postponement of marriage allows a growth period between the parental home and the connubial one. Others are very sure of themselves— what they want and who they are—by twenty-one. As long as marriage, or intimacy, is not permanently avoided, delaying the age at which a man or woman enters marriage may be positive. Not only do those who marry in their late teens and early twenties have higher divorce rates, they also have higher suicide rates. (By contrast, in every other age group, marrieds have the *lowest* suicide rates, compared to those who are divorced, widowed, or never-married.) Since financial discord is a major contributing factor to divorce, waiting until one or both partners have achieved economic stability may improve that couple's chances for successful marriage.

Monica, who is now forty-seven, was a transitional single until she was forty-one. Since Monica always knew that she did not fear intimacy but had simply not met the right one, she made the most of her single years. Still, Monica recalls that others were unable to accept her prolonged singleness. At a Sunday afternoon barbecue, I asked Monica what it was like for her when she was single. "I once went to a dude ranch," Monica explained. "I guess it was about fifteen or eighteen years ago, so I was about thirty-two at the time. There were four of us sitting around the table; three women and a man. Everyone but me had been divorced. The man asked me my age and if I had ever been married and after I told him no, he said, 'Boy, you must be a real loser.' Since then, I've heard he's been divorced two more times!

"Being single wasn't the pits for me," Monica continued. "But it got to a point where I would work out a little story. I'd say that I'd been married at eighteen and it was annulled after two months. 'It's as if it never happened,' I would add. That explained why I was still single, but at least I'd been married. I'm glad I waited until forty-one to get married. But I don't know if I would like to be single still. My former roommate is, and I think the last few years have been very hard for her." Since Monica had had a hysterectomy, and her husband was divorced and had children by his first marriage, childbearing was neither the reason she gave up singleness nor a problem for her in marrying so late. Monica simply decided to settle down "because I finally found someone I could love, and I didn't want to grow old alone," she confided.

For the transitional single, conventional intimacy eventually wins out. By marrying, the transitional single enters the mainstream of the adult population. Singleness was a "phase"; coupling will, usually, last longer than those unmarried years. But what about those men and women who are permanently single? Are they single by choice or by default? This is where confusion is revealed, for often these men and women cannot decide whether they chose singleness or if it "just happened."

Who are some of these never-married men and women?

Ramon, a lawyer in his early seventies, attributes his single status to economics. "I never managed to make enough money to cope with Jewish middle-class standards." He meets new

**53**

people through friends and "personal charm." Ramon describes his life as "totally busy." He found that working hard was a "great antidote to loneliness, and TV and radio give me someone to talk to."

"I don't want to get married or have children," says Bill, a thirty-five-year-old orthodontist who lives in Los Angeles. "I like being my own boss. I work every other week and still make fifty-thousand dollars a year. I like to go skiing and motorcycling—the outdoorsy stuff. Most of my relationships with women last a year. I refuse to be pushed into marriage; I don't see any disadvantages to being single."

Barbara is a fifty-five-year-old school nurse who lives outside Chicago in her own home. During the summers, she travels. From the age of twenty to thirty, she had an affair with a married man. After that relationship ended, she dated quite a bit, but she gradually settled into a reclusive life-style.

Mel, a forty-year-old academic, has lived in Trenton, New Jersey, for the last two years. He has five reasons for his prolonged singleness: "I didn't marry out of college because I couldn't find a girl to share my dream of getting a Ph.D. Then I didn't marry in graduate school because so many of my friends were getting divorced or having affairs, I began to have serious doubts about the rewards of marriage. After graduate school, I didn't marry because I became involved in doing research and publishing my first book. Then, I lost my job due to a budget cut and had to abandon my social circle and move to Trenton. Now I'm single in Trenton because it's a bad place for a single person to be. It's hard for me to find dates here. But I'm not lazy. If I met someone in New York or Philadelphia, I would commute on weekends."

Wayne, a physician in his late thirties, earns over $100,000 a year. He lives alone in his house in upstate New York and has a small, community practice. A friend who had Wayne to dinner explained: "He got up at least nine times during the meal to take calls. Then he had to leave in the middle of dessert to deliver a baby. I'm sure it must be hard for him to find someone willing to put up with a life that has so many interruptions and such long working hours. All Wayne meets at the hospital are nineteen-year-old nurses, and that's not what he wants."

"I don't want to get married for at least twenty years," says Vicky, a twenty-three-year-old black college junior. "And I'm not sure I'll even marry then. I want to go to graduate school and I can't commit myself to two things at once. On two separate occasions, I lived with guys, and it was the same old chauvinistic thing. I made breakfast and I did the cleaning. They walked around with blinders, as if love conquers all."

Are these singles unmarried by choice or by default? With time the answer may be a little of both. An unwilling single at twenty-three may by forty-five, for example, espouse a commitment to singleness as a defense. "At forty-three, I guess I'm committed about being single," a woman from Syracuse, who works as a bookkeeper and flies her own small plane, told me. Likewise, a committed single at thirty may by fifty be an unwilling single if his or her singleness has not proved satisfactory. "I always thought I'd be married by now," a man in his mid-forties, who moved back home with his father in the last year, told me. This man, renowned for the singles parties he used to throw with his ex-roommate—who married and had a child—finds he now longs for a wife and children.

Some unwilling singles, embittered by their inability to find "the one," fail to live their lives to the full. They resent their singleness, long for marriage, and live in the worst of both worlds—not enjoying the advantages of singleness and lacking the fruits of intimacy. Linda, for example, is thirty-five years old and has wanted to be married since her early twenties. Yet she has never even come close to getting a proposal. She resents her singleness—when she was younger it was more fun, but now that she is older she is frightened by the continuing pattern. "I can tell you about the quality of *my* life," Linda begins, "but for a more typical single's life in New York you have to go to the upper East Side or to someone who's renting a house on Fire Island. You'll find a single swinger there. My life tends to be *extraordinarily* quiet. I don't know. When I lived a single life in California with a bunch of other singles the quality of my life there was very different. I lived with roommates. I entertained. I saw myself as a single who was going to enjoy being single, who dated, who was looking for a husband, who figured sooner or later she would fall in love and get married. And who didn't take her work very seriously. It was just a way to pay the rent. In a way, it was a very adolescent approach to life—even though I was closer to thirty than I was to twenty. I put off a lot of things saying, 'I'm not going to do them now, I'm going to do them when I get married.' Nothing seemed to be fun unless I was doing it with a man. I was very socially active. I had a lot of people around me. I don't know. In some ways, it might have been somewhat narcissistic. It wasn't California, it's me. I've chosen to live a somewhat reclusive life here." Linda buries herself in her job, has one close girlfriend, and is socially and sexually cut off from men. She found she was unable to attract the type of men that she fantasized about. "I'd rather be alone than 'settle,'" she explained.

Of the many singles I encountered, Linda was one of the few who saw her reasons for being single as very personal ones. "I'm single because I'm too wrapped up in my own life," Linda explained. "I don't have enough to bring to a relationship. I don't think I could do it justice." Did she think that feeling secure in oneself was essential to a good relationship? "Yes," Linda said. "I think it's unfair and I think it's counterproductive to go into a relationship with the hopes that the other person is going to solve your problems. I don't believe in doing that to someone else. But I'm closer to solving my problems now than I was two years ago."

Others are unable or unwilling to verbalize an awareness that their singleness is linked with their inability to share with someone else, but their actions demonstrate that this is the case. A thirty-two-year-old single woman, for example, sees her married boyfriend each weekday morning for half an hour; they have had this arrangement for the past five years. She is satisfied with the relationship; "Doug is the best friend I've ever had," she explains. "I've never been closer with anyone." Phil, who is thirty-four, was obese for the first twenty-four years of his life. Although he has been thin for the past eight years, he is still a "fat man inside" and finds the thought of loving a woman very frightening. "I've been seeing the same woman on weekends for the past year," he told me. "It's the closest relationship I've ever had and sometimes it scares me." Warren, a thirty-two-year-old singer, has been "dating," as he put it, "one of my employers for the past eight months. I finally wanted to take the plunge and move in together, but she panicked and said she wasn't ready. We worked it out though, and we're still dating." Warren, who finds women who either push him too far or on whom he makes excessive demands, has yet to live with someone for more than a weekend. For him, even "dating" the same woman for eight months is a step closer to intimacy.

Women in their thirties and forties gave concern about childbearing as a reason why singleness gradually lost its appeal. "I still want to have a child," an artist in her early forties told me, "and when I think of my age, I get frightened." Those unmarried women who wanted children told me that they feared it would never happen, since they had not yet even found a mate. Although they had enjoyed being single, they did not want to be single parents. One freelance writer in her mid-thirties, who has six brothers and sisters and believes strongly in the family, pinpointed her ambivalence about this aspect of being single: "My mother didn't have her first child till she was twenty-eight and she was still having children into her forties. I decided only in the past few months that I would like to get married. The deepest joys, I believe, come only through family and children. They don't come through career, I discovered, and they don't come through travel."

Another woman, an attractive graphic designer, also shared her fear at being thirty-two and unmarried. Her anxiety is so great that she persistently scares men away as she forces relationships, racing against her childbearing clock. Rather than focusing on the quality of her relationship with a man, she has told me that she thinks in terms of, "Is he the one? Does he want to marry me? Would he make a good father?"

Are there ramifications to permanent singleness? Committed singles think not. "I've never really thought deeply about the pros and cons of being single," a Chicago woman in her forties told me. "I feel I'm too young-minded right now to settle down, or settle period. I've been everywhere, I've done everything. I have no regrets." A California man in his mid-thirties told me, "No one's demonstrated to me a good reason for marriage." Why is he single? "I was born this way, and it's very natural," he replied.

In contrast, unwilling singles think that never marrying is hazardous to their physical and emotional health. "I wouldn't weigh two hundred pounds if my boyfriend had married me," a woman of thirty explained. "Sometimes I'm so lonely I don't know how I get through the night," she continued. "I'm lonely," says a saleswoman

**59**

in her early thirties. "I want to be with someone so I can give and receive love. I spend a major portion of my income on trying to meet men—singles weekends, summer homes, going out weekday nights, eating out."

In a journal article, Margaret Adams notes that there are three essential criteria for successful singleness: "the capacity and opportunity to be economically self-supporting"; "social and psychological autonomy"; and "a clearly thought-through intent to remain single by preference rather than by default of being requested in marriage, either as first venture or following widowhood and divorce." Although Adams addresses herself to the single woman, I have found those comments equally applicable to the single man.

I found that those never-married men and women who accepted singleness—and achieved all of Adams's criteria for positive singleness—soon left that state. Perhaps the internal resolution of their singleness makes them more attractive partners? Social scientists Elaine Walster and G. William Walster note that the quality that makes a person most appealing to the opposite sex is the ability to relax. Certainly reaching a point of comfort about one's singleness would aid in achieving a relaxed air. Phyllis, for example, spent half an hour with me extolling the joys of singleness and living alone. A few months later, I learned, Phyllis, who is thirty-nine, had moved in with her boyfriend, a separated man in his forties, and set up a joint household.

When someone mentions the "single population," few automatically think of the unwed mother or the growing number of unwed fathers. Yet, like celibate clergy and gay singles, the single parent is a distinct category of the unmarried population. "Are you single?" I asked a man of thirty. "No, I'm a single parent," he replied. My interviews with unwed parents confirmed that, for the majority, social concerns are lower in their list of priorities than child and job. Forty-year-old Carol sees her boyfriend, the father of her child, on a daily basis; he works close to Carol's apartment. Since he supports Carol financially she can afford to be a full-time mother. For most unwed mothers, parenting and making ends meet take priority over mate-hunting.

Who are the single parents? Steve, one single un-married father whom I met, lives in Brooklyn with his ten-year-old daughter. The mother of his child was living with another man at the time that she became pregnant with Steve's daughter. Steve gained custody of his child and, still living at home with his mother, has chosen to raise her alone. He thoroughly enjoys being a father, but vows never to marry. "I grew up wanting to have a child and not to marry," Steve said at a meeting of single parents. "Every time my mother saw a married man, she would say to me, 'There goes another sucker.' I think all women are 'single parents' in that the burden of childrearing falls on them. But that situation will change in this country. Men have paid a tremendous price for not having had a more active role in parenting."

The very young never-married parent is a special type of single with special needs. Half of all out-of-wedlock pregnancies occur within six months of the start of sexual activity. Fortunately, programs are emerging around the country to provide counseling for the unwed parent.

Through adoption, foster care, born out-of-wedlock,

or A.I.D. (artificial insemination by donor), there is now, also, a growing number of older unwed parents. These single parents are deliberately bringing up children because, as one thirty-eight-year-old woman told me, "I planned for a full year to get pregnant. I knew I would never marry, but I wanted to be a mother. Then I got pregnant. Did I make the right decision? Look at this baby. What do you think?"

For articificial insemination, sperm may be provided by someone known to the woman, or it may be donated anonymously. What are the legal complications that may arise from A.I.D.? One case that came to the public's attention was a New Jersey single who was artificially inseminated by her boyfriend; in 1976, a court ruled that the father was entitled to visit his child, but that he also had a responsibility to support him. Of the ten to twenty thousand artificial-insemination-by-donor births each year, no one is sure how many are born to single women. A.I.D. is a secretive process, for the protection of mother, child, and physician. But many clinics have seen an increase in the number of single women who want A.I.D. The fee, which ranges from $75 to $100, discourages those with vague motives. Some infertility clinics have policies that prohibit A.I.D. for unmarried patients. Notwithstanding obstacles, there are lesbians and career women in their thirties who are afraid that they will not meet a man and marry before their childbearing years are over, who opt for A.I.D. It provides them with what they perceive as their last chance to become mothers and also allows them to be impregnated by someone whose genetic background has been verified by a clinic.

Another relatively new phenomenon is the increase

in adoptions by older unwed men and women. Although it is estimated that there are no more than several thousand singles throughout the country who have adopted, it is a definite trend. I asked a friend of mine, with whom I had gone to college, if she had ever thought of adopting a child. "Yes," she answered, "I did plan to adopt a child. I really like children, but I knew I couldn't deal with the social pressure of having a child out of wedlock." If a single man or woman adopts a child, it is still "out of wedlock," but the stigma is not as bad as it is for the woman who bears an illegitimate child. Most adopting never-married men and women state that because there are so many unwanted children already born, they prefer not to add to the population problem or ignore the needs of those unclaimed youngsters by having their own children. Their main motivation is having a child to love; whether or not it is biologically theirs is unimportant to them.

Another part of the heterogeneous never-married population that is neglected in the media discussion of the "single" are the celibate members of religious orders. According to the census they are single, but they do not define themselves in that way. During the Middle Ages, when the male population was depleted by the Crusades, poor single women had a choice of living at home, working on the land, or working as spinners (the source of the word *spinster*). Their upper-class never-married counterparts could enter the religious life. (Indeed, many older nuns were widows.) Today, religious orders still offer men and women a way to remain single, but the Roman Catholic clergy has changed. Priests and nuns, more often than not, dress like the people whom they serve. In all but sexual matters, they are being granted more freedoms than ever before.

Like the transitional single who ultimately enters the world of the married, not all men and women who join the church remain. Some depart it to embark on a life that includes sexual contact. Nina, a forty-one-year-old sister, told me that of the forty women with whom she entered the convent, only eleven or twelve are still nuns; the rest are either career women or married with children. For centuries, the convent, the church, and the monastery have had an appeal for certain women and men. Nuns, priests, and monks go through a rigorous training and few people would discount the dedicated and valuable services that they perform.

It seems odd to consider these members of religious orders as "singles." Are they? Clyde is now in his mid-forties; up until five years ago—from the time he was seventeen—he was a monk. Clyde, who has several advanced degrees and has taught in universities throughout the South, now feels that the chance to get a good, private higher education was his primary motivation for entering the monastery. "I was rather typical in that I joined right after high school and stayed for fifteen years," he explains from his urban apartment. "Through therapy, I realized that I wanted to try to please my mother very much—mother church, mother religion, mother mother." Did he consider himself single as a monk? "No," he exclaimed, "not the way I see single now. In a monastery, you had a very controlled environment. You were part of a community. There's a loss of individuality. Now I feel that to be a single man means to be free. I'm single now; I wasn't single then."

Nina, who is still in her order, disagrees. She feels that religious life has stressed individuality to her. But she, too, has never seen herself as single. "The best way that I can explain why I became a nun is that it was a calling," she said over lunch. "I really believe that marriage is a vocation, given what you need to be a good mother or a good wife. In the same way, if you are called to be a single person, you need special qualities to help you deal with all that being single entails— loneliness, aloneness, working things out for yourself. I feel that a religious vocation is a calling from God to live in this particular style. In no way does it mean a rejection of people." Over the years, Nina has questioned her choice of the religious life but "mainly in my thirties. I think it was a part of that age. I grew from the questioning. And I'm glad I'm still in religious life; please God that I always will be." But every choice— religious life, marriage, permanent singleness—means a road not taken. "In religious life, you give up a lot," Nina continued, "but you also have a lot of benefits. I don't have to worry about who cooks. And I don't have to wake up every morning to a screaming child."

Still another group of never-married men and women who do not consider themselves single are homosexuals. ("People still think of me as single, even though I'm not," a musician in her twenties, who lives with another woman, explains. "My dear, I'm not single," Jerry, a gay playwright told me, "I'm gay.") There appears to be a growth of homosexuality on college campuses and in the under-thirty-five age group. Whether this is real or a reflection of the fact that homosexuality is more out in the open is subject to debate. Certainly there has been a growth of homosexual organizations, many catering to the young, such as the Gay Academic Union and the National Gay Student Center. For some, homosexuality is a form of sexual experimentation. Several never-married men and women in their early thirties told me that they had had homosexual experiences in their early twenties but had resolved the conflict and now wanted a conventional, heterosexual marriage. For others, homosexuality becomes a permanent way of life.

Just as there are never-married heterosexuals who live alone and who cohabitate, there are homosexuals who live alone (and participate in a "tribal" gay life) or who live together as if married. Recently there has been a plethora of literature about the homosexual community; I will not attempt to summarize it here. For the purposes of this study, the salient point is that although homosexuals are technically single, most see themselves as members of the gay community. Unlike the heterosexual single—who is usually in the never-never land of being an outsider in a predominantly married society—homosexuals socialize in a world that is tightly knit and cohesive.

Gays who do not have a network of gay friends and lovers, or whose one lover leaves, experience the same kind of loneliness and depression that often characterizes the single life of heterosexuals. One man I interviewed was distraught and confused when his lover of twenty years left him. He was hurt by how little compassion anyone showed him, as if the pain would not be so great because he was gay.

Jerry, the gay playwright and novelist, told me that

**66**

he knows nothing about lesbians because lesbians and gays do not get along. "There is a matrix," he explained. "Other than with their own, lesbians get along best with straight women. Second best with straight men. And last with gay men. Gay men get along best with straight women, next best with straight men, and least of all with gay women."

The majority of the estimated 10 to 20 million homosexuals in the United States today are tabulated as never-marrieds, even if their life-style replicates a one-to-one marital type of living arrangement. Brendan, a thirty-two-year-old never-married homosexual, has been living with his divorced lover for three years. They moved to New York from their small hometown in Oklahoma, "because we could never have lived together back home," he told me. "As long as nothing is confirmed, our families can still think that we're just roommates. Our closest friends know that we're gay, but no one at work knows." Sue, who is "legally and socially considered single, but I'm not," has lived for seven years "with another women in a long-term lover/friend relationship" in a metropolitan area. "I have always been a lesbian and a feminist," Sue, who is assistant director of a social service agency, tells me.

There are many cases—not yet reflected in the statistics—of separated or divorced men and women who are now homosexual. I know a thirty-year-old woman who has been married twice and is presently separated from her second husband. She has a ten-year-old child, and is a lesbian. She found the women's center in her community provided her with peer support as she moved in the direction of a permanent separation from her second husband. She does not want to remarry; she wants to live alone. At this point, she does not feel her homosexuality was a cause of her marital breakup. "I don't want external circumstances to account for my next relationship," she explains. "I want a relationship in which both of us are willing to work on ourselves, and on the relationship, share even the difficult things, have our own strength as individuals, and share that strength with each other. More equality, more mutuality."

Jerry has been married twice and has fathered three sons. He divorced his first wife after twenty years and has been separated from his second wife for the last ten years. During the first marriage, Jerry had numerous mistresses, a fact he harbors a great deal of guilt about. He had a few homosexual experiences—the first one at the age of thirty-two with an elevator boy at a hotel where he was a guest. Since 1969, he has not touched a woman. He is thoroughly enmeshed in the gay subculture. Since Jerry "came out of the closet," he has also shifted the focus of his writing career to novels, nonfiction, and plays about the gay's world.

Jerry firmly believes that he should have been gay all his adult years. If he had been, he would have avoided hurting the women he had tried to love in his marriages and extramarital affairs. Jerry enjoys the solitude and independence of living alone, but he also finds his network of gay friends—and the lovers who come in and out of his life—an antidote to loneliness. He finds gay love more congenial to his own temperament. It is "more diffuse and gentler. There is a certain ease of forgiveness." Jerry lives in a tribal gay culture, rather than a gay "married" arrangement, in that he has intermittent lovers and is not tied to any one person.

All three of Jerry's sons are straight. Two live in Alaska, and he does not see them very often. The third, the youngest, lives in an apartment directly below Jerry's. His son mixes with Jerry's gay friends, although there is some rivalry for affection and attention when Jerry's lovers are in the same room with his son. Jerry thinks there are a lot of gay married men who are living dual lives. "They go to the baths and leave their wedding bands with the rest of their jewelry so no one knows." He believes that many gays who will not come out of the closet and live openly drink themselves to death, commit suicide, and go from bad marriage to bad marriage. He feels that he is a completely different person since he turned gay and wishes it had characterized his entire adult life. Why is he gay? "My dear," he replied, "women are fine, but men are better."

# 4

⇢⇢⇢⇢⇢⇢⇢⇢

# *Single by Decree:*
# *The Once-married*

Probably no social topics receive as much attention in the popular press today as marriage and its counterpart, divorce. No matter how much advice is offered on enduring the trauma of divorce, it is still a painful process that entails a considerable readjustment for those who experience it. Marital breakups have consequences not just for the partners involved, but for their families, their employers, and the community at large.

Even if they were married only briefly, separated or divorced people will always be considered "once married" in government statistics; in psychological make-up they will never again resemble unmarried singles. The effects of an unsuccessful marriage are seldom benign, and many significant measurements—mental health, suicide rates, income, admission to hospitals, frequency of car accidents, physical fitness—indicate that once-married singles do not fare as well as their never-married counterparts.

Not one divorced person that I interviewed wanted to return to his or her former spouse. By contrast, many separated singles still hoped that they might reunite with their estranged partner. Singleness will for only one out of eight who divorce become a permanent life-style. For the others, it will be a transitional state lasting, on average, three to seven years. Thus, divorce does not generally appear to be a renunciation of marriage, but rather a rejection of a certain partner at a certain time. "I never doubted that marriage and family was a more natural way of life for me," a graphic designer in his early forties, who remarried four years after his divorce, told me. "I just needed to find the right person to fulfill those goals." "Right after my divorce," a re-married store owner in his late forties told me, "I set out to find a woman who would provide the companionship that marriage gives me." Those, however, who write off all the apples and the barrel as well will not remarry. "I don't think I can live with a man," a woman in her forties, who had been divorced for twenty years, told me. "I'm a loner, I suppose." A divorced high school teacher who is cautious about all new relationships commented: "Beautiful as she was, she was a nightmare to live with. I'm leery of attractive women now, but I'm not interested in homely ones. So I don't see an alternative to living alone."

Two-thirds of those who separate get divorced within a year. One out of every ten separated couples takes over four years to divorce. Since "separated singles" may declare themselves married on their income tax returns or to the census bureau, it is almost impossible to estimate how many of them exist in this country. According to the census bureau, 4.6 percent of all American men and women over the age of fourteen in 1978 were separated.

Separation thrusts a man or woman into a new set of social, financial, psychological, and physical circumstances. Regardless of whether *he* left or was left, whether *she* dreaded or relished the anticipated change, the separated single is still tied to the past. "Until last week," a separated man of fifty, who had been married eleven years, told me, "I was living in a lovely house with my wife and two children. Now I'm living in a furnished room in a hotel three blocks from our home. This separation is really destroying me." His work has suffered; his judgments are questionable. A woman of twenty-three, who had been married three years, told me how her separation affected her. "I was the one who told *him* to move out," she explained. "I was the one who changed the locks. I was the one who wanted the marriage to end. My actions were necessary because of the way he treated me throughout our marriage. Since I threw him out he hasn't called once to ask if we can try again. He's happy to be rid of me. I can't work. I can't think. I'm running everywhere. I just want to keep busy—and with new people who don't know me as a married lady."

A dress designer in his mid-thirties, who had been married for two years, told me: "I considered myself divorced as of last August third, when my wife moved out."

"But are you legally divorced?" I asked.

"No," he answered. "But that doesn't matter. We're legally separated, and that's as good as divorced."

Legally, separation may be the first step toward divorce, but emotionally, separation and divorce are very far apart. Separation is a sudden, shattering trauma. The greater the emotional and financial dependence on the former spouse, the graver the initial impact of the split. Considering that wages for working women are 57 percent of men's average pay (most of the separated women I interviewed reported incomes between $3,000 and $12,000 a year), the separated single woman has very real immediate financial problems. Separated men, especially those with children, who are conscientious about supporting two households, are overburdened by extra expenses. "I have little incentive left to work," a separated man told me. "Almost half my paycheck goes to my wife and children, even though her parents have more money than I'll ever see." (This man's former lack of financial responsibility for his family was a major source of marital discord. An outside agency now mandates that responsibility.)

Marion, who is forty-two, has been separated for ten weeks from her husband of twenty-one years. She earns about $500 a month as a part-time publicist; she considers it pin money. With three teenage daughters, a house in the suburbs, and expensive tastes in clothing, she is concerned about the financial consequences of her upcoming divorce. To assure herself the best economic settlement, she watches her every move—refusing dates and avoiding, as far as possible, being seen in public with any man—so that her husband (who walked out on her) will have minimal grounds for a divorce countersuit.

The separated man or woman, like the widower or widow, goes through stages of grief, but his or her mourning is received in a very different way. Relatives and friends rarely rally round the "new" single. Even those who do offer support undermine it with comments like, "I know you'll get back together again" or "You're lucky to be out of it" or "I don't know how he put up with you this long." Some separated men and women prefer not to talk about their breakup in the hope of a possible reconciliation. The more that relatives, friends, and business associates are involved, the more likely that the dissolution will be permanent. One woman received a "Congratulations on your separation" card about a month after her separation; it was the last time she had a date with that particular suitor.

The separated single, unlike the widow or widower, can still contact his or her former partner. The struggle to remain apart—and out of contact—is a continual one. In moments of loneliness, guilt, depression, euphoria, or boredom, it is all too tempting to renew contact with the separated mate, thereby prolonging the healing process.

Why do some separated singles delay their divorce? One women in her early thirties, Barbara, has been separated from her husband of nine years for four years. For the first three years of her separation, Barbara lived with a man. For the last year, she has lived alone in her own apartment. She has a master's degree in social work and is employed in a social service agency. For the past six months she has been a member of a group of divorced and separated women who meet once every other week to discuss career problems. "I would say my husband is one of the first people I would call if I had a problem," she told me over lunch. "We're very good friends. Being in touch with him doesn't interfere with my current social life. For one thing, he lives in another city. I have no fantasies about ever wanting to get back together with him. We talk about our social lives. It wasn't like this when we first split up. There was a lot of pain then. But it has been four years. The divorce papers are in; we've just never pushed it. I don't feel any need to rush. I like him. I liked him when I was married to him. I still like him as a person. I just didn't want to be married to him anymore."

The separated status is a bridge between the security of the past marriage and the unknown world of the single, and as such provides the separated single with a certain psychological stability. Therapist Anne Rosberger, who directs the Bereavement and Loss Center of New York, confirms this. "For the partner who didn't want the separation," Rosberger said in an interview, "there's always hope. The one who sought the separation isn't always so quick to pursue the divorce because he or she may have a psychological need to remain in limbo and enjoy the freedom without any commitment or responsibility, but feel secure in the knowledge that the spouse is available and the marriage can be resumed. It's like the married woman who can behave in a very seductive manner because she is safe. She has the security and protection of a marriage on which she can always fall back."

It is well known that many live-in relationships involving separated men and women break up once the separated single is divorced and hence legally free to

marry. In this situation the relationship blossomed because it offered the same guarantees that dating a
married man (or woman) offers the single adult—involvement and intimacy without the risk of commitment. A professor in his fifties, who had been separated
from his wife of fourteen years for the past three years,
explained, "The only reason I'm not divorced is that
my lawyer was disbarred during the proceedings. His
disbarment had nothing to do with my case. But I
think of myself as divorced. I'm now living with a lady.
We wouldn't be married even if I were divorced." The
numbers suggest that if he ever divorced, they wouldn't
even be living together.

What about those men and women who are going
through a separation period that *is* leading to a divorce?
The significant phenomenon that I repeatedly found in
interviewing those separated for under a year was the
compulsive need to talk about one's spouse. No matter
what the subject, the marital partner became part of
the conversation. One man, who had been separated for
three months, began our conversation with "My mother-
in-law called me yesterday; right after that, my sister-
in-law called. I saw my wife yesterday. I think you
should know that I'm married, although I'm separated
and really divorced." I suddenly realized why an article
by Judi McMahon in *New York* magazine about placing
an ad in the newspaper to find prospective dates sug-
gested stating clearly, "No recent separatees, please."

But the opposite reaction to a separation—one or both
parties being unable to discuss the marital breakup with
anyone—can also occur. As in bereavement, this is far
less common than the compulsive need to relive the
marriage or separation. Inability to talk about the

former spouse indicates a repression of the mourning, and a consequent delay in the recovery process. Although the separatee who compulsively relives the marriage breakup may be placing an enormous short-term burden on friends, he or she will probably realize greater long-term benefits than the separated person who licks his wounds in silence—and continues to do so for a protracted period. Perhaps that is why so many bars are filled with recent separatees—these places offer a milieu in which grievances can be aired with perfect strangers, and longer-term relationships are not burdened with this temporary loss of verbal control.

As journalists Erica Abeel and Susan Braudy amply documented in their autobiographies of their own separations, and as my interviews confirmed, the period immediately following a separation is one of confusion, frenzy, and definite action. The fulfillment of sexual fantasy that often occurs is most noticeable. One man, for example, explained that he felt he was looking only for "one-night stands" because he was afraid of getting involved, and getting hurt, too soon. A woman, after her marriage of almost thirty years terminated, found she was going to bed with anyone and everyone. "I started dating," she explained, "but I was sick at myself. Every man that I went to bed with I couldn't stand by the second date. But I had sex every day for one month after my husband and I separated. You see, I never had sex with anyone but my husband and I never could imagine it with anyone else." Another woman, who separated at twenty-seven after seven years of marriage, went out on her first date just two weeks after she left her husband. "For the first six months," she explains, "I got involved with four men, one right after the other.

It was as if I was on a merry-go-round, chasing the brass ring. It was a horrible time in my life. It really wouldn't have mattered if it was four men or four hundred. I just hated myself at that point. I felt so disgusting." Typically, this behavior lasts from six months to one year following the physical separation. Often, the actual divorce decree marks a return to traditional mores and brings about a rethinking of the rules and long-term roles in a relationship.

Many, upon reflection, evaluate the actions they took immediately following their separation as positive ones. A singer who separated after nine years of marriage immediately lost forty pounds and went back to performing. A minister, who had a parish for fifteen years in a medium-sized California coastal city, listed the changes that followed his separation: "I put up my own art (my wife didn't like any of the paintings I had bought; I had to keep them in my study); I related better to my daughters; I didn't have to deal with my father-in-law; I learned I could make it on my own; I got out of a rut; I moved into a beach house with a view of the water; and I immediately discovered who were my friends, who were my enemies, and who couldn't give a damn about me."

The positive actions following separation are often in directions previously proposed by the spouse. If a husband (or live-in boyfriend) had complained that a woman did not dress very well, she may, following separation, find herself buying new outfits and becoming more fashion conscious. Had the wife complained that the husband was too miserly, the separated husband may let the dollars flow. The vacation that a couple fought over for years because it seemed too expensive may suddenly, and impulsively, be taken by one of the separated partners. The duration of these changes varies according to the individual. A woman who dressed poorly may buy a few outfits immediately after the initial separation, but within a few weeks or months she may be back to her old habits. A miserly man may find that the emotional trauma of constant spending far exceeds the "revenge fantasies" fulfilled by his initial change of habits. Indeed, eight years following her separation, one divorced woman, who made a list of the positive responses she had had to her separation, wondered why she had failed to continue these major steps forward. The benefits of her renewed sense of independence, weight loss, cultural interests, and an improved self-image were gradually undermined as new liaisons reinforced, rather than diverged from, the pattern of her unsatisfactory first marriage.

Twelve weeks after her separation, forty-two-year-old Marion—whose twenty-one-year marriage was described earlier in this chapter—spoke to me about her outlook following the second month of her separation. "I couldn't accept the fact that I was separated. I was doing my *shiva* number. But now I've come to see the reality of it. I've been married since I was sixteen, really. I have a good time now whether I go out with my girl-friends—married or single—or couples. But what's happened is that I'm a lot friendlier to everybody now. I'll talk to the doorman. And I'll talk to people in a restaurant. Not with an ulterior motive, but because I feel something that was stifled is coming out. I had this one relationship that lasted more than twenty-five years. I don't think anything can stun me again the way that I've been stunned."

A frequent reaction to a separation is to go back to a "first love." One twenty-two-year-old woman, within a week of asking her husband to move out of their apartment, called up and asked out the man to whom she had lost her virginity seven years before. He was still single, and they went out to dinner. Over the next few months, he provided her with a lot of friendship, some sex, but primarily an outlet for her need for intimacy with a familiar person. So common a pattern is this seeking out of old boyfriends or girlfriends that it was the theme of the 1979 movie *Old Boyfriends*. Upon her marital breakup, the heroine takes her high school and college diaries and travels cross-country pursuing the men she had loved; one had died in the Vietnam War, another owned a formal-rental business, and another was divorced and living with his daughter. The movie had a happy ending—she reunited with her ex-college sweetheart, who had become a once-married single parent. In real life, however, I found that these old relationships, rekindled during the separation period, rarely last. The initial comfort to be found in them is soon undermined by a recurrence of the problems and dissatisfactions that led to their collapse the first time around. One California man, after his seven-year marriage dissolved, began courting his high school sweetheart. Because she lived across the continent in New York, it took over a year for her to reconclude that the diary entries she had made so many years before were accurate descriptions of the ambivalence and frustrations that the boyfriend, older but remarkably unchanged, still evoked in her. Linda, a thirty-one-year-old art director, returned to her first love after her short marriage terminated. Her boyfriend, "my first, complete, utter love," had also recently separated from his wife. "When he called me," she explained, "he was traumatized because his wife had gone off with her lover. He sent me a ticket to fly to the coast for a week. It wasn't a perfect time, but it was close to it. We were very compatible. I was willing to give it a try. I was really crushed when he wasn't interested."

Why do separated men and women often seek out those with whom they had close relationships in the past, or want to call the lover, live-in, or mate from whom they just separated? Is it out of a wish to reconcile? I asked that question in a self-help group for those going through separation and divorce. The majority opinion was, "It's loneliness."

Obviously not all separations lead to divorce; it is estimated that one-sixth of separated couples do reconcile. Separation can be for those individuals a time of growth and introspection, a period of self-evaluation and development that enables their marriage to be better the "second time around." That is the theme of Victoria Yurasits's inspirational article, "Does Separation Have to Mean Divorce?" "Six months later, after several phone calls and dates—a period of learning to get to know each other again—my husband and I resumed sleeping in our old double bed" and her ten-year marriage not only survived the separation, but was better for it. Reconciled separatees, however, tend to adhere to the rules of privacy governing marriage, and few outside the immediate family know about the temporary interruption in the regular cohabitational routine. I found that recently separated couples more readily seek the confidential help of a psychiatrist than confide in good friends or more distant relatives.

Newly separated or divorced wives are often very ill informed about their status. Courses on marriage and divorce, given at adult education centers, sometimes provide enough information to alleviate the confusion and fear that usually surround the demise of a marriage. These courses usually cover such topics as: grounds for divorce; custody and visitation; financial concerns—alimony, child support, payment of legal fees; and property rights (protecting them during marriage and getting a fair portion from the divorce). Cynthia, a forty-year-old New Jersey housewife who took such a course, found the information that she gained was particularly important. Without a career of her own, and with a high cost of living, she was destined to be a poverty-level "displaced homemaker," after twenty-five years of marriage, unless she knew what her legal and financial rights were. At the time she began the course, Cynthia was represented by her husband's attorney; she had accepted her husband's advice that she did not need legal counsel of her own. Several other members of the class had already been granted divorces and were shocked to learn how ill informed they were and how inadequate their property settlements had been.

Sudden singleness has a devastating impact. Even men and women who immediately enter a new intimate relationship may find they need help dealing with internal conflicts about an ex-spouse or about their new role as single parents. Self-help groups for the separated and divorced have proliferated in the last five years. I attended a meeting of such a group in Queens, New York. Led by a psychiatric social worker, this group explored the deeper conflicts activated by separation, as well as the practical problems such as finances, babysitters, and meeting new people. Separated, divorced, and widowed women, ranging in age from twenty-eight to forty-five, were present. They were all single parents. One of the women, a thin, attractive mother of a three-year-old, had been separated for two months. "When she first came to the group," another member explained to me, "she was a mess. She wasn't even combing her hair. She didn't seem to want to live. She had a storybook marriage. She and her husband were high school sweethearts. They were married for seven years before they had their child. Then one day, supposedly without any warning, he walked out on her. He doesn't want to talk to her or to reconcile. He just wants out."

In 1979, there were 8.8 million divorced men and women in the United States and 96.5 million who were married. It *is* true that "everybody's doing it, doing it" —getting divorced—but what they're doing after it is remarrying—again and again. The United States has one of the highest divorce rates in the industrialized world, but it also has one of the highest rates for marriage.

Once separation becomes permanent—the divorce is final—what do divorced men and women tend to do? Initially, divorced singles feel compelled to blame their ex-spouse for the breakup. This "blaming syndrome" is unfortunate, since it discourages self-examination. Without honest introspection, repetition of previous mistakes—in dating, in relationships, in a second marriage—is all too likely. The divorced single experiences pain and anguish, and their absence may have far-reaching effects (in that the first marriage is unresolved, future relationships suffer). "I was married for seven months when I was twenty-four," a divorced man told me, brushing aside the impact of his marriage—and divorce. "But that was ages ago. She didn't really matter." He is now thirty and recently gave up his apartment to return home to his parents.

If emotional difficulties brought about a divorce, and they are left unresolved, they will probably taint later relationships. A man in his early thirties, who had been divorced from his wife of three years for more than seven years, still spoke to me of her with disdain. He could not even recall the qualities that had initially attracted him to her. None of the women he had taken out since his divorce did he in fact like. Since his divorce, he had flitted from one short-lived romance to another. His job record indicated the same pattern.

A divorced friend, now forty-five, met her ex-husband when she was twenty-seven and he was twenty-five. "We were no spring chickens," she explains. Her description of her marriage was a typical war story. Because they have two children, and her ex-husband lives across the street with his new wife and baby, she has to deal with him more often than is usual for divorced women. In the dozen years since they parted she has not resolved, or come to terms with, her anger. In each phone call with him, she relives all the old frustrations. It is a difficult situation for everyone—her children, her ex-husband, his wife, and her boyfriend. Is she planning to marry the man she has been seeing for the last six years? "If I did," she says, "I would have to move to New Jersey to live with him. I just can't bring myself to give up this apartment. What if it didn't work out? I would never again be able to get a two-bedroom in Manhattan for what I am now paying." (Six months later, she called to tell me she had sublet her apartment and was living with her boyfriend.)

One women told me about a friend on the West Coast whose attitude toward remarriage changed drastically: "After she broke up with her husband I was worried about her. Her first letters were about how desperate she was to marry again, and I was afraid that she was so shaken up by being single that she would jump into the next relationship that came along. Then she went through a whole bunch of unsatisfying affairs. Now she has no inclination to remarry. She doesn't need the security. She's done a hell of a lot of growing. Perhaps, because the pressures are different, when you become single, you change. About a year ago she met someone and they're still together. She seems content with the relationship just the way it is."

Unable instantly to form satisfactory relationships with the opposite sex, many divorced singles fall into the same pattern that I observed in never-married singles—they immerse themselves in their work. Women, with or without children, may be motivated by the financial pressures that are now all too real. Even for them, excessively long working hours may be less a function of their job than of their need to have a socially acceptable way of dealing with their aloneness. For example, a man in his late thirties, a divorced Irish Catholic, changed his schedule at the printing plant where he works so that he would be on from nine P.M. till five A.M. on weekends. He thus eliminated even the possibility of a weekend date (or a weekend alone). Another forty-five-year-old twice divorced man works seven days a week, from two in the afternoon till midnight, at one job. He awakens at ten and barely has time to dress and eat breakfast before he is off to his second job as a mental health therapist. A twenty-two-year-old divorced artist works night and day, without a break, so she will not have to risk intimacy. Many divorced singles enroll in college and graduate programs to fill up their newly acquired free evenings and weekends. Of course some do it to *meet* people, and some must return to school to gain the skills that will increase their earning capacity, but it is used by some as an extra professional obligation to consume the enormous amount of free time suddenly thrust upon them.

There is one cliché that I would dispute—that one should wait several years after a divorce to commit oneself to a new relationship (although marriage on the rebound is not advisable). I discovered that those who made an emotional commitment within two to four years of the divorce were more likely to remarry—or to maintain a new long-term relationship—than those who dated furiously or retreated into their shell. This is also borne out statistically—most remarriages occur for women within the first six years after a divorce and for men within the first three years. I asked a friend, a divorced editor, how long it had taken until she found the man she has been happily living with since 1973. "Let's see," she said, "I have to count since my separation. That was in April and I met him in December."

Separated and divorced singles tend to view marriage in one of two ways: either with overwhelming repugnance or with overzealous romanticism. One divorced woman in her early thirties described love: "Fairy tales, bells ring," she said. "Fireworks go off. I am capable of very intense feelings and I believed that when you are in love, that love relationship would always be the same. That notion totally wiped out the possibility for me of an honest marriage." Another woman expressed the opposite view: "I think that all men will treat me like my husband treated me. My first marriage was a living hell and I doubt a second one would be any different. The romance dies in a few weeks and then it's day-to-day boredom." Another woman, who has been divorced for four years and is now thirty-four, recalled her marriage to her "first love." "We met when I was twenty-one and we were married for seven years. But I was a basketball wife. I didn't really have a profession or even a job. I was just his companion. He was such a great guy—a super person—and I always loved him. I trusted him absolutely." But he left her for another woman. Her next boyfriend also left her and married someone else. She floundered for another two years before finding a new concept of love and marriage. Recently, she wrote to me that she is dating someone steadily and hopes marriage and childbearing are on the horizon.

Some single men and women voiced their preference for dating divorced, rather than never-married singles—especially if the former had no children—because the divorced single has had the experience of making a commitment to another person. A separated woman in her early thirties explained: "I've reached a point in meeting men that if they tell me they've never married —unless they have lived with someone for a long time— I lose interest in them. I can pick them out! I can almost say who has been married, who hasn't been married, whether they had children or not." Younger single men and women found divorced singles far too bitter about marriage—even half a decade or more after the dissolution of a first marriage—to be appealing.

The most desperate once-married singles I found were the childless divorced women in their mid-thirties to early forties who still wanted to bear children. Frantically, they searched for a new mate so they might fulfill their parenting dreams before it is too late. "The baby issue is still something I want to explore," explains a once-married public affairs director. "I'm thirty-six, so time is short." She is "pushing" the marriage question with a man she has been dating for the past year.

In England, there seems to be a trend of older women who are dating, and marrying, younger men. Since 1964, this trend has increased, and from 12 to 15 percent of all marriages there display this age difference. It is simply a matter of supply and demand; in England there are 800,000 more males in the prime marriage years—twenty to twenty-four—than there are females, and they are marrying divorcées and single older women. In the United States, a similar dating trend has been noted among older women. In many instances, however, marriage does not ensue. As one woman in her forties told me, "I prefer men in their twenties. They don't put any pressure on me, and in many ways I find them more sexually and intellectually stimulating than men my own age."

"I like dating men in their late twenties," a thirty-year-old divorcée said. "If they haven't been married, it's still okay. I feel younger, and more girlish, when I'm with younger men. They seem still to have so much spirit and enthusiasm. The older men, especially the ones who are divorced and have alimony and child-support payments, feel as if they've 'done it all.' I have my life ahead of me and I want to be with a man who feels the same way."

The growth of single parenting is a problematical development in our culture. It is a complicated and stressful situation for men as well as women. During the last decade, there was a 60 percent increase in the number of children of all socioeconomic groups who lived in a single-parent household. The number of divorced single mothers tripled, while the number of divorced fathers with exclusive child custody increased by only 1 percent. It is estimated that nearly half of all children born in 1977 will spend a notable period before the age of eighteen in a single-parent household, probably the mother's.

"At my daughter's sweet sixteen," a separated woman told me, "only two girls out of fourteen had parents who were still living together." Raising a child in a joyful household with two parents is an ideal that most advocate, but few suggest that an unhappy household is better than a single-parent one. Since 60 percent of divorced fathers default on their child-support payments within the first year after divorce—and only 2 percent of all divorced women with children receive more than $5,000 a year in support—how do single divorced mothers cope? Some survive as best they can on public assistance; others work their way up from low-paying jobs; and still others depend on parents, or remarry as soon as possible. A thirty-eight-year-old divorced woman named Clare is very proud of the way she handled her marital breakup and entry into the work world: "In February, my husband and I decided to separate. He moved out by April first. By June, my house was sold. I packed up a ten-room house all by myself, found an apartment, and by July fourth my kids were at camp. I went to Fire Island that weekend to unwind and the next week I was in the city looking for a job. I started off at one hundred and forty dollars a week, no degree, no business background, and now, four years later, I'm making fourteen thousand dollars a year. I've moved up to middle management. I'm not a secretary anymore. I will even be getting a secretary of my own."

The single mother's concentration on her financial plight may, however, diminish her appeal. As one man who had dated twenty divorced women with children told me, "All they do is talk about their financial predicament. I can empathize with them, because it is a real problem and that's what they are most concerned about, but it really makes it difficult to start a relationship. Usually they aren't even aware of how obsessively they dwell on their poverty."

Single fathers with only visitation rights also suffer because of the breakup of the family. A thirty-three-year-old executive, who sees his six-year-old child once every two weeks, cites the minimal contact with his son as the most difficult part of being single again. "I miss my child very much. There is a great satisfaction in being a full-time father and when this is denied, both father and child lose out. I resent the fact that most single fathers become fast-food dads to their children. We have to plan how to spend a day, how to entertain, and educate a child for a short time, whether it be a day or an evening. I don't consider that parenting." He advocates joint custody, whereby the child is equally shared. (Few courts, however, believe such a system is in the best interests of the child, since it represents too great a disruption in school and home life.) A photographer in his late thirties, who has been separated for three years, visits his young daughters three or four weekends each month. Being away from day-to-day contact with his children is the most difficult part of being single for him.

There are notable differences between divorced singles with and without children. First, and foremost, children often necessitate prolonged contact with the ex-spouse. The need to separate, and put the past behind, is at cross-purposes with the need to permit the ex-spouse to have continued contact with the children. A divorced Texas businessman found that when he visited his three children and saw his ex-wife, his hopes of reconciliation were continually revived. "Finally," he explained, "I had to give up the dream of getting back together when my ex-wife got pregnant and married someone else."

Some once-married singles lean on their children too heavily for the emotional support that should come from a new relationship and never develop enough inner strength to handle their loneliness, or singleness. One divorced woman even finds herself sleeping with her ten-year-old daughter "more often than I know is good." Instead of learning to go out alone, these singles take their children along, even when the children might be better off in bed.

Once-married single parents also find that their dating activities are severely hampered by the demands that children make. June has been married and divorced twice. Her first marriage, at the age of twenty, lasted five years. With her second husband she had one child, who is now ten years old. How would June compare dating as a single person to dating as a single parent? "It's two different activities," the petite, thirty-six-year-old office worker told me. "For me, dating as a single parent is often more trouble than it's worth. It's the babysitter. Just the thought, 'Do I want to go out after a day of working and hassling with my daughter?' It's tiring. My current boyfriend took out two opera subscriptions last year. But there are times that—as much as I love opera—I just resent the whole bothersome thing of dating. If you are lucky enough to get a sitter, your whole evening revolves around when the sitter has to be home. Dating as a childless person may be a pain as well, but you don't have these practical considerations."

Single parents who are too embittered by their first marriage to seek a new relationship may find that children provide enough emotional comfort, and a good excuse, to avoid the singles scene. "It is more difficult being single if you have a child," a thirty-five-year-old woman explains, "but my child has provided me with the companionship that many singles lack. She has also given me a sense of stability and joy." Older once-married women, whose children have left to live on their own, also look back on their single parenting years as their best ones. "I most enjoyed living with my sons," explains a fifty-five-year-old journalist who now lives alone. "We were temperamentally suited." The empty-nest syndrome, however, is particularly stressful for these once-married single parents. "I raised two wonderful daughters," a fifty-four-year-old divorced business executive explains. "My marriage lasted only nine years. I was never lonely when my daughters were around. But they've been on their own since 1969. By then, I just couldn't see myself with anyone day and night after so many years without a man."

June and the other single mothers I interviewed all agreed that a full-time housekeeper and babysitter would facilitate dating. All the single fathers I interviewed were able to afford this luxury, or else had their mothers close by and willing to babysit. If possible, women will arrange babysitting cooperatives, in which each woman is responsible for several children once or twice a week and is free the remaining evenings. Yet, even if babysitting is provided, the lack of spontaneity in a single parent's dating life is a restriction. Patricia, a single parent who has a one-year-old child, wanted to accompany her friend to a singles bar right after their class was over. But when she called her babysitter she discovered he wanted to leave shortly. Reluctantly, she returned home. Most married mothers with a one-year-old child find that they also spend most evenings at home, but for Patricia, going out at night is a crucial part of her social life.

One group that is affected by divorce and deserves further study is the parents of once-married singles. As a widow of seventy told me, "Doesn't anyone care about what my son's divorce meant to me? It took me eight years to adjust to my first daughter-in-law. Then, all of a sudden, he divorced her and within a year he was remarried. But what about my relationship with his first wife? Do I just cut off *my* feelings because he's cut off his?" A woman of fifty-five, whose daughter had divorced her husband after three years—they did not have children—was very clear in how she now felt about her ex-son-in-law. "I hate him," she said. The father of a childless divorced woman expressed a similar view about his ex-son-in-law. "As far as I'm concerned," he told me, "he's dead." Other parents, no matter how much time has elapsed since a son's or daughter's divorce, do not abandon hope that the offspring will remarry. "Last night when I said my prayers over the candles," a fifty-eight-year-old mother of a divorced woman who has been single for eight years told me, "I prayed that my daughter would find someone who would love and support her."

Despite the popularity of divorce, failure in marriage, like failure in business, is frowned upon in our culture. Until they remarry, divorced singles feel they must continually show how much their lives have improved since their divorce. "Look at how well I'm doing" summarizes the image they try to project. Overtly or internally, they are apologizing for their marital misjudgment. It may be fortunate that the horror of separation and divorce inhibit the once-married single from rushing after only a few months into a new and permanent tie. But when temporary caution about relations becomes permanent fear of all possible romantic encounters, chances for a fulfilling remarriage are diminished. Most once-married singles, I found, are in search of a second chance with "the right one." (Remarried men and women, I was pleased to learn, report that they really "work at" their relationships. They appreciate how dear intimacy is, for they have known an unsatisfactory union.) A reevaluation of one's behavior in a relationship is the key to a more fulfilling life after divorce. Those who apportion blame and cling to the past administer their own punishment. Those who learn from the experience grow, and increase the likelihood of achieving a balanced life, whether shared or not.

# 5

# Single by Chance:
# The Widowed

A thirty-five-year-old woman whom I interviewed shared with me her experience of dating a widower in his fifties. "He was too old for me," she explained, "but he had a warmth that made him delightful. He put his cards on the table. He found living alone unpleasant. Having a companion was important to him. He married late in life and still had his teenage children living with him. He was a lovely guy. He had no hang-ups. 'I really want a wife,' he said. He stopped seeing me because he didn't want me to be his wife. There was no hurt. I was just too young for him. It was so nice going out with someone like that rather than with someone who doesn't know if he even wants to be part of a couple. I just find widows and widowers to be more attractive human beings."

Some of the "attractiveness" of widowed persons

stems from the fact that, as a group, they are more perceptive about themselves than the majority of other singles. They know what they want, whether it be remarriage or continued singleness. I found that a widow or widower would get to the nuts and bolts of his or her singleness in just one brief conversation. He or she could pinpoint the drawbacks and advantages of singleness without the defensiveness of those who have never married or the bitterness of those who were separated or divorced. If remarriage was desired, the widow or widower would express the hope that the new spouse would come along. But rather than just hoping for the event, or debating the merits of aloneness versus togetherness, time and energy were invested in finding that second (or third) spouse.

An economics professor told me about his secretary, a widow in her fifties. Approximately one year after her husband of twenty-five years had died, she announced to her boss that she was taking a month or two off to "find a new husband." In the weeks that followed she had dates every day. She went to parties. She traveled. She joined singles groups. She may have overdone it a bit, but when she came back to work, she had a new last name. A forty-four-year-old childless widower, whose wife had died the year before, stated, "I'm a happily married man who's between wives." When he met "the right one," after three months of dating, he proved the truth of his statement.

In the United States, one out of every six women over the age of twenty-six is a widow. In 1979, there were 10.5 million widows and almost 2 million widowers. These suddenly single adults are of all age groups and

97

classes, although the majority are elderly. Their singleness is quite different from the singleness of the never-married or the once-married person.

Mrs. Berman, a sixty-year-old office worker, was grief-stricken when her husband of thirty-five years died of a heart attack. They had been so close during their marriage that, as her daughter put it, "She never went to the bathroom without him being nearby." At Mr. Berman's funeral his widow screamed, "Ben, how could you do this to me? You promised we would go together." Mrs. Berman's health, not the best in any event, deteriorated during the ensuing months. But after ten months, she seemed to be improving—adjusting to her singleness by cultivating female friendships and staying with one of her three children at least three nights a week. She was even planning a trip to Spain with a group of women. Yet, less than a year after her husband's death, Mrs. Berman died too. The cause of death, according to the death certificate, was a heart attack. Perhaps the heart attack referred to was that of her husband.

Other widows and widowers, like the key character in Mark Twain's short story "A Californian's Tale," deal with their loss through temporary mental aberrations. In Twain's tale, the Californian reenacts each and every year the return of his wife, who disappeared twenty years before. His faithful friends humor him, put him to bed, and after that time of year passes he is always somewhat better. When the husband in Nancy Hale's short story "The Rider Was Lost" learns of his wife's death, he refuses his friend's advice that he's " 'still got a lot to live for.' " Speaking slowly, with desperation in his voice, he chants, "I want my wife. I want my wife."

A widower who is thirty-six told me that, after two years, he felt himself completely recovered from his wife's death (she died suddenly at thirty of a heart condition). His voice, however, had a forced joviality. "I couldn't sit around feeling sorry for myself because of our daughter," he explained. "I think if not for her I would have taken longer to recover. But she was only three at the time and there were too many immediate concerns for me to dwell on the meaning of life or any of that nonsense."

Sally, a widow who was twenty-six at the time her husband was killed by a robber, took over four years to get back on her feet. Sally too had children—she was pregnant at the time of her husband's murder and also had a two-year-old—but it was necessary for her, temporarily, to move back with her parents. For the first year after her loss, Sally was on medication. She also spent two years in therapy. "Then it was time to go on," Sally told me. "But it was not for another three years that I came around enough even to think about dating again. Then I realized that I was still young. I was a woman. I had sexual needs. The best years of my life turned out also to be the most tragic. But it was time to go on and start a new life."

Colin Murray Parkes, in *Bereavement*, pinpoints the following predictable phases of adult mourning:

1. Shock, numbness, denial, disbelief.

2. Pining, yearning, and depression.

3. Emancipation from the loved one and readjustment to the new environment.

4. Identity reconstruction.

At what stage will the widow or widower seek out help? "Interestingly, most people who are bereaved do not come to us right after the death, due to the nature of the bereavement process," therapist Anne Rosberger explained. "In the early part of bereavement, people generally do well. They're sad and they feel terrible, but there is a certain kind of numbness that insulates them and permits them to do things in a way that they will never be able to again, until they resolve the whole grief process. Usually, three or four months after the death, you get people calling. 'My mother was doing magnificently,' the caller will say. 'She was getting about and doing all kinds of things and all of a sudden she seems to be getting worse. She's going backwards.' " Rosberger explained that the widow or widower is not really going backwards—he or she is going forwards. "The full impact of the death has become so real that the initial protective shell is no longer adequate. At that point, widows and widowers start to do things which they think are strange. Or they get depressed. But those are all normal aspects of bereavement."

Dr. Phyllis Rolfe Silverman of Harvard University found that widows and widowers could provide a good deal of help for each other. In the program she devised, one widowed person serves as a contact for another, the idea being that someone who has had the same experience can provide the needed compassion and practical information. Services such as these, when available, are of aid to those widows and widowers who are unable to resolve their grief alone. But the majority of widows and widowers must, and do, make the necessary adjustments to their new status without outside help.

**100**

A Canadian journalist, widowed for seven years, epit-
omized the view of the widows and widowers whom
I interviewed. "I'm neither fish nor fowl," she wrote to
me. "I'm not married, but I'm not single either. I live
in a no-man's-land." A widower in his thirties, when
asked if he was married or single, replied, "Neither;
I'm widowed." A young widow with two toddlers re-
marks that she feels stigmatized because she is a widow,
not because she is single. "I don't even tell people that
I'm a widow anymore," she explains. "I say I'm a single
parent. That way I don't get the pity and the sad faces."
Twenty years ago when a woman's romantic life was
thought to end with widowhood, pity and sad faces
might have been her only solace.

Loss of identity is one of the major problems facing
the widow or widower, particularly the older bereaved
spouse who has no vocation or who is retired, and even
those with active careers, such as the fifty-eight-year-
old Canadian journalist, suffer some loss of identity
when a spouse dies. "My life is unreal," she writes. "My
work is real. The rest of my life is just acted out. It's
a pretense, and I wear a mask of indifference. Inside, I
know that this is not *me*. I keep thinking that things
will change, and I will resume a man/woman life again.
But seven years have passed. I'm happy to think that
this unreal existence won't be true for the younger
generation when they are my age. They'll be better
trained, organized, prepared to live in the world alone.
They won't be appendages of a man." It is a common
solace to assume that the next generation will do better
with their lives. Luckily, the next generation will also
have that solace. Sociologist Helena Znaniecka Lopata
studied one thousand widows in the Chicago area. Her

results echo the loss of identity theme: ". . . [the widow's] identity as a wife is shattered and there is no comfortable role of widow available to her [in our culture] as it is to widows in other parts of the world. In addition, she often needs to 'make herself over,' from a dependent person, living vicariously through the husband and children, into an independent person."

While those who are divorced are sometimes thought "failures" at marriage, the widowed do not labor under that additional handicap. It is generally assumed that theirs were satisfactory marriages. In groups that combine widows and divorced single women I found that, initially, the once-married women were jealous of the widows' "higher" status. The widow is accorded sympathy and comforted by the familial support system. She need not apologize for or explain away a marriage that did not work. The widows, however, often found the sympathy given them interfered with their new lives. "I got tired of the looks whenever I said that I was a widow," one woman explained. "I wanted to be accepted or rejected on the basis of what I was, not what I had been."

Researchers have rated the death of a spouse as the number one stress that one can experience in life—greater than divorce, jail, or job loss. In the first year of widowhood, widows consult physicians with three times the frequency of a comparable married population. The suicide rate of widows and widowers is higher than for any other group of single or married people. Even in the second year following the loss, widows and widowers have a higher mortality rate from health-related causes than would be expected in a comparable married population. As the numbness of grief wears off, and the relatives and friends evince less interest in the bereaved, the practical problems of isolation, lower income, and a "roleless role"—as sociologist Starr Roxanne Hiltz refers to widowhood—assume a more prominent place.

Widows with jobs in which to immerse themselves tend to do better than widows whose identity was solely that of wife and mother. Overwork is a common danger for new widowers, but diminished enthusiasm for a job can also occur. "I used to really care about my job," a young widower told me. "I'd be in the office by eight and although I'd be home by six, I would bring work back from the office. But after my wife died, I decided that work wasn't all that important. I value things differently now." A few widowers told me that they seek escape either in mood-altering drugs (alcohol, Valium, marijuana, etc.) or in casual sexual liaisons.

How long a bereaved man or woman will remain single is largely dependent upon his or her age. There are five times as many widows as widowers over the age of sixty-five. "And the widowers don't want us," a widow of sixty-five told me. "They want a woman who is twenty years younger. So, do I go out with a man who is twenty years older than I, or just give up?" Another widow of seventy-three cried when her friend tried to comfort her by telling her that she would soon be living in an apartment house with other widows. "But I'm not used to a world of women," she moaned. The younger widow does not have this problem. There are more men available. "I know a forty-five-year-old woman who was determined to remarry," a sixty-year-old woman who had been widowed for nine years told me. "Right after the funeral, practically, she started hunting for another husband. She had been married twenty-five years, but she didn't want to be alone. Within six months, she had found a new husband." Was that because she didn't really love her first husband? "Not necessarily," explained another fifty-five-year-old widow. "Some women just feel less comfortable being alone. They need a man more. I don't want to remarry, but I would like to have some platonic male friends, just to go with me to the theater or to a movie or to dinner. The trouble is, they want either to go to bed with you on the second date or to marry you."

The older widow, either retired or having never worked, has the problem of filling her daytime hours; the younger widow, who either works or has children at home, has to occupy her evenings. Many senior citizens activities clubs for women are comprised almost exclusively of widows. "Some women literally go from one group to another," the director of an almost all-widow crafts program told me. "Monday they'll be at the Y lectures. Tuesday they'll go to a group that meets at a synagogue. Wednesday they'll go to another group that meets in a church, and so on. The groups are almost all nonsectarian regardless of where they meet."

Frances, a sixty-year-old widow whose husband has been dead for two years, found that the best way to meet men was through the dances sponsored by her synagogue. "I'm old-fashioned," she told me. "I still think you should wait to go to bed with a man. So I won't go home with someone the night that I meet him. I'll give him my phone number and ask him to call. But if I like him, we'll have sex by the third or fourth date." She does not want to remarry but she likes sex. "I married my husband when I was twenty-one. I met him when I was fifteen, and ever since, he was the 'one.' But it was the Depression times so we waited to get married. I was a virgin when I got married. I don't have to tell you how few of them there are today." Her sister, who lives in the same building, and has been a widow for nine years, does not communicate very often with her. Frances commented, "She doesn't like my life-style. She prefers to go out only with women. But I like men."

Other older widows echo Frances's reluctance to enter into another marriage. Beverly, sixty years old, does not want to remarry. However, she enjoys the company of men "if someone takes me out, and we spend some time together, and I feel comfortable, then it's okay to have sex." "I had two opportunities," related a sixty-five-year-old woman who had just retired from her secretarial job at an advertising agency. "But they couldn't give me anything that I can't give myself. I have a lot of friends. I play bridge twice a week, and I go to movies." Another widow I spoke with, aged sixty, has her husband's pension and does not need to marry for economic security. "I think I would prefer to live with a man than to marry him," she explained. "There would be fewer problems with wills and children and all that." Another widow, who is seventy-two and lives in a rural Pennsylvania community, would marry but "it is difficult to find a congenial, vital male in my age group," as she puts it. "I'd prefer a mate—one with like interests. I've been a widow for eleven years." Until the right one comes along, she keeps busy with her thirty-four grandchildren, who visit her frequently. She is also active in growing her own organic vegetables and baking cookies. "I had a good marriage," another widow told me, "but things are not so bad now."

That woman, who is sixty-six, also does not want to remarry. "My housekeeper and I moved into the city and we now share an apartment with my daughter, who is single, and a doctor. She's very busy, but we do have meals together. And I have my volunteer work and my friends."

Although loneliness was the major personal problem cited by widows and widowers that I interviewed, there are also practical considerations that the bereaved find difficult to adjust to. Young widows with children generally need monetary or day care help to run a household single-handed; older widows who have relied on their husbands for balancing the checkbook and paying the bills need financial counseling or aid. Widowers with children—and in 1976 the nearly 2 million widowers in the United States had some 174,000 children below the age of eighteen living with them—are in the same predicament as the divorced father with custody. They quickly remarry, learn how to cope with running a household alone, or hire nannies.

The young widows that I interviewed, in contrast to the separated singles, described the first year following the death of their spouse as a period of depression and diminished sexual interest (in contrast to the frenzied sexuality of the separated single). Young widows with children have a more relaxed attitude toward the possibility of remarriage than divorced women with children. "It would be nice," they say, "but the children come first." Although none of those I interviewed expressed the view that an overactive social life might be considered disrespectful to her dead spouse, that appeared to be an underlying reason for their controlled approach to dating. After a period of mourning of variable length, young widows begin to see themselves as unattached women, capable of forming new relationships. Margaret, a registered nurse, was widowed at the age of twenty-nine; her husband, who was then thirty-two, died of cancer after a five-year illness. Eight years later, she remarried. What were people's reactions when, a year after the death, she began dating again? "People really didn't say too much," she explained. "Fortunately. By that time, I had relocated from the Midwest to New Jersey. None of my friends in New Jersey even knew my late husband. The one exception was my late husband's father. He was quite outspoken and, 'As far as I'm concerned,' he said, 'you'll always belong to Paul.' I've never forgotten that statement. It really took some sorting out and understanding on my part to grasp why he might have felt that way. But that was the only negative reaction that I got." Her focus for the next few years was on raising her three young children and on returning to school for refresher courses so she could reenter the nursing profession. Time permitting, she went out on dates, but not during the week—she was too tired. She met her second husband when visiting her sister-in-law. At church one Sunday morning her sister-in-law pointed out a man whose wife had died of cancer the year before. "We got married about a year later," says Margaret. "We combined households—he had three grown children of his own. I won't say we haven't had some minor adjustment problems, but on the whole I'm amazed at how well it has worked out."

Unlike the divorced, who are often bitter, the widowed are sad. Although many novels and movies contain the theme that new partners can never overcome the cherished memory of the dead spouse, I did not find that to be the case with those I interviewed. Those who did not want to remarry were quite clear in their reasons for wanting to remain single—freedom and self-sufficiency. Those who wanted to remarry but could not find a suitable mate were also practical about the limitations of their age. Those who wanted to remarry, and did, were able to reconcile past memories with their new relationships. "My life is not better now," one young widow told me. "I had a good marriage and I know we'd still be married if my husband had not died. But this is my new life. It's strange. I'm introducing my boyfriend to many of the friends who knew me in college and were at my wedding. But they're happy for me. Most of them like George, and he's great with the kids. I'm hoping we'll be getting married within two years."

Another difference between the divorced and the bereaved single is the latter's continued contact with the deceased spouse's family. Mary, whose husband of two years died when he fell from a boat, is closer to her first mother-in-law than she is to the mother of her second husband, to whom she has been married twice as long. In neither marriage were there any children. In cases where there are children, relations are actively nurtured by both the bereaved spouse and the in-laws, even after the remarriage. (Sometimes the divorced daughter-in-law or son-in-law maintains a close bond with the former in-laws, but this is rare.) The widowed usually continue to wear their wedding bands and, until remarriage, to retain their married names.

The widower or widow is forced to overhaul his or her life completely. The speed with which this exacting task is accomplished varies greatly. Does the support offered by one's immediate circle hasten or retard this process? The need for support differs as much as does the way in which the bereaved resolve their mourning. Susan, whose husband died when she was eight months pregnant, was given enormous support from her siblings, parents, and in-laws. Yet, eight months after her husband's death, she found it necessary to begin seeing a counselor because she felt that her need for support was increasing rather than decreasing, and that she had to find the inner strength to stand on her own. Ben, by contrast, was offered little support from his closest relatives and friends after his wife died. Since his need for help was far less than Susan's, he managed to resolve his sense of loss and, within just a few months, had moved on to an acceptance of his new single life-style. Therapist Anne Rosberger finds that those closest to the bereaved are often the most impatient. They expect her or him to create an instant new life. Rosberger, who has counseled hundreds of widows and widowers, says, "It's not as if the widowed don't want to have this new life. It's just that it's very very difficult. Where does an older person meet friends? In the supermarket? In the singles bars? 'Make a new life for yourself,' people say, as if you can hail a new life as you hail a cab. 'I want a new life.' Do you buy it? But where do you buy it?" Eventually, the widowed single *must* make that new life. For them, no marital reconciliation is possible. Many widowed persons told me that their dead spouses appear in their dreams, and that this was comforting, but their wishes are futile.

In the year and a half since her husband of fifty-three years died, Charlotte, who is seventy-seven, has tried to move on. "I keep active all day so the evening isn't so long," Charlotte explains. "I try to invite people over. My son-in-law's mother, who's eighty-four, stayed with me recently. And my sister from Florida, who's eighty-three, came for a week. I also cook special meals for my grandchildren, who live close by, and give them a weekly allowance, so they [want to] visit once a week. But it's a responsibility, especially looking after older people who are handicapped. So, in a way, I'm glad when they leave. I'm free again, but I'm also alone." Charlotte, who looks twenty years younger than her age, is fine—until she thinks about her husband. Then the tears fill her eyes and she feels an indescribable loss. "I watch very little TV because I can't watch anything sad. And I can't listen to sad music. I miss the walks my husband and I used to take after dinner. I'm too afraid to go out alone after dark. I'm in bed by eight at night."

Bereaved parents, like their divorced and never-married counterparts, have to guard against overattachment to their children. Society accepts the tightly knit family that is bereft of one parent. As hard as it is to explain divorce to a child, telling a five-year-old that his father or mother will never be returning home inevitably leaves one feeling inadequate to the task. Sally, whose husband was killed, found that when her father-in-law died five years later, death became an obsession for her five-year-old son. "He wants to know why only men have died," she told me, "and if he's going to be next." Eda LeShan has written a sensitive book about a parent's death, to be read by youngsters. But can any book provide comfort to Sally, or her children, when she prohibits them from playing with guns "because your daddy was killed with a gun"?

THE WIDOWED

We have come a long way from throwing widows on the funeral pyre, as was the practice in India, or forcing them to enter convents, as was common in the Middle Ages. Nonetheless, the widow or widower has as many stereotypes to confront as the never-married or the once-married single. If the never-married is the "swinger" and the once-married is the "loser," then the widowed is the "martyr." As Lynn Caine so aptly described it in *Widow*, "Now I had a new role. Widow. And I was going to play it magnificently. Make way, Jackie Kennedy."

The widowed population will grow by the end of the century as the baby-boom adults reach old age. Since life expectancy for women is, on average, four years longer than for men, unless women begin to marry younger men, social customs condemn many of them to some interval of elderly widowhood. Do widows and widowers relish singleness? Initially, they have no choice. "I hate being single, but I refuse to compromise by entering into a marriage just for security or sex," one widow wrote to me. She had never thought she would be single again. Typically, she does not see herself in the same class as never-married or once-married singles, even though their problems are similar. "The last three years were the best ones in my whole life," a woman of thirty-two, whose forty-four-year-old husband had recently died of a heart attack, said. "My baby and I will make it together," she continued.

Some widows and widowers make the most of their single years, whether they remarry or not. "I am content to live a quiet life," says a sixty-six-year-old retired typist who has been widowed for thirteen years. "I have many friends in my apartment house and I have the freedom to come and go as I please." "My ninety-three-year-old grandfather has been widowed for seventeen years," a friend told me. "He's had a lot of women interested in him, but he's content to live alone in Florida. He's a rather tame and sedate man who has known marriage and all types of singleness. His first marriage did not occur till he was in his thirties; he divorced three years later. He remarried soon after that; this time it lasted thirty-five years." Others are as miserable to be single as those who divorced bitterly or who could not find the "right one." A widower in his forties refused even to think about what it had been like for him after his wife's death. "I gave that all up eighteen months ago when I remarried," he told me.

It is often said that friends and relatives besiege the widowed person with potential mates. After I interviewed the widowed, I began to understand why. They lack the ambivalence about relationships that clouds the personal goals of so many unattached singles. By and large, the widowed have a "couples" mentality and honor the institution of marriage. They have, indeed, remained with their mates till death did them part.

# 6

⇢⟩⟩-⟩⟩⟩-⟩⟩⟩

# *Single by Single:*
# *Living Together*

Today, when someone says "I do," the next question should probably be, "Do what?" Traditional marriage is just one option for intimacy; living together is another. There are essentially three styles of living together: (1) A dating pattern in which one participant spends a number of nights per week at the other's abode, this I shall call a pseudo Living-Together-Arrangement (a pseudo-LTA). (2) A trial marriage, in which a common household is maintained as a possible prelude to marriage. (3) An alternative relationship to marriage, in which a common household is maintained, without formal vows said or planned. Except for that "piece of paper," this arrangement is the same as marriage.

I found that young never-married singles and once-married singles (who were recently separated or determined not to remarry) were more frequently engaged in pseudo-LTAs. Trial marriages were practiced by older, never-marrieds in their late twenties and thirties. Alternative relationships to marriage were most often entered into by older once-marrieds from their thirties up through their eighties.

Instances of all these types of cohabitation have increased in the United States in the past decade. Between 1970 and 1978, for example, the number of "households which contained two unrelated adults of opposite sexes" increased more than eight times—to 1.1 million households, according to the census bureau. (It is probable that more couples than that live together. It has been estimated that between 6.5 million and 20 million persons currently live together outside marriage. Because living together requires neither application to, nor license from, the state, government statistics relating to cohabitation—those cited in this book—are consistently low.) The number of family households grew by 10 percent from 1970 to 1977, while the number of households comprised of unrelated persons increased by nearly 50 percent. (It is estimated that there are 100,000 group-living situations [communes] today, including at least 750 "intentional communities," cooperative households with formal names and definite organizing principles. These arrangements differ radically from one-to-one relationships.)

There is little available documentation about living-together arrangements (LTAs) in America today. The census bureau statistics are approximations. There have been some sociological studies on the living-together habits of the college-age populations, but cohabitation extends far beyond the campus.

Why do men and women live together rather than

marry? Those in pseudo-LTAs cited the possibility of sex, avoidance of loneliness, insecurity, adherence to the "new morality," peer pressure, and the wish to learn how to be close to someone of the opposite sex. Those in trial marriages expressed the belief that living together would test the viability of a successful marriage; those in an alternative relationship to marriage seemed to want to appear unconventional, feared commitment, felt bitterness toward marriage (once-marrieds), gave reasons (separation, for example) for being unable to legalize the union, and/or started living with their partner and found they preferred that arrangement to marriage.

The pseudo-LTA takes many different forms. It can consist of the couple who occasionally spend the night together, or the relationship that resembles trial marriage, but in which separate households are kept. The common characteristic of all pseudo-LTAs is the avoidance of any marital commitment. "I've lived with at least ten men in the past ten years," a divorced woman in her thirties confided. "Carl kept his own apartment, but he was here practically every night and on weekends. I cooked and cleaned as if I was his wife, but now, looking back, I realize it was not a real relationship. I was just playing house. Then there was Dorian. He traveled a lot so we stayed at his apartment whenever he was in town. My work suffered. Phone calls went unanswered since I would sometimes fail to check my service for days at a time. Now I feel as if I was little more than his mistress, even though we were both single."

Joel lived in a pseudo-LTA when he was a nineteen-year-old college sophomore. "There were five of us—

three men and two women. We all shared partners. I kept my room at the dorm, but I basically lived in my friend's house for six months. Everything revolved around sex. I don't think I got to know anyone on a deeper level, but I must admit, I needed that kind of arrangement at that time in my life."

Joel's comments pinpoint one of the most dangerous aspects of the pseudo-LTA—it is mistakenly thought of as a "close" relationship. There is frequently a marked difference in the ways that the partners described their involvement in the relationship. Generally, one partner had substantially more invested in the relationship than the other. I wondered whether pseudo-LTAs concealed an inability to love, or a fear of commitment, but found that those who went from one pseudo-LTA to another could not offer much insight into why they needed this type of relationship. "I lived with someone for two years, but she kept her own apartment," a single man in his early thirties told me. "I don't know if I'd do it again. Breaking up is a lot worse when you have to take your clothes back."

Even though these pseudo-living-together arrangements do not mirror marriage, those who had experienced them believed that they had tried marriage. Also, some adults reacted strongly to the dissolution of such a relationship, blaming the fact that they had lived with their partner rather than themselves or the partner him- or herself. Margaret, a thirty-year-old bank clerk, described her live-in situation as marriage, even though she still maintained her own apartment. "I lived with my boyfriend for four years," she says, "and I enjoyed the relationship very much. However, I found myself giving much more than I was getting. I like the married type of relationship we had, but I believe we started taking each other for granted." Stan described to me his two-month liaison. He enjoyed the marital setting "but since the relationship lacked substance, we broke up. Still, I learned quite a lot about myself through the experience." Stan is a thirty-three-year-old never-married accountant; he now feels he is ready to find someone to whom he can make a permanent commitment. Wayne, a twenty-seven-year-old security guard, lived with a woman for almost a year, but she kept her own apartment "in case things didn't work out." "We had some good times and some bad times," Wayne notes. "I simply felt too restricted. The feeling that I had responsibility for another person was a hassle, but I would probably do it again, with the right person."

Obviously it is how the living-together experience is viewed—as well as an honest realization that it is not usually the same as marriage—that determines how each partner benefits from it. More often than not, cohabitants in short-term liaisons, or when a second residence is maintained as a safety valve, learn more about themselves than they do about marriage, per se. As one twenty-eight-year-old black student explained, "The lady I lived with in 1976 really helped me get my head together after I had been in the army for five years." Cohabitation can sometimes be the interim arrangement that stills a never-married single's fears about marriage, making a permanent commitment feasible. "I'm glad I lived with Sid," Gladys, a thirty-two-year-old actress, told me. "It was the first time I ever made that much of a commitment to any man. True, I kept my own apartment. But I was at his place practically every day and on weekends. And we stayed together a complete year. But now I know that I really want to get married and have children. I want a family. I'm not as afraid of being close to someone as I used to be. Sid helped me learn how much I'm capable of giving to a man."

But an unsuccessful pseudo-LTA can permanently dissuade a single from seeking a lasting, intimate love relationship. A twenty-nine-year-old Washington, D.C., woman has lived with two men—one in graduate school and the other for nine months after she had moved to Washington. "These bad experiences," she explained, "have had an enduring effect on me. They have made it difficult for me to live with someone new. Because of those traumatic experiments, I have decided to live alone. One of my boyfriends was so unstable that months of tenderness became hell and I had to seek psychiatric help." That woman, like many who have repeatedly failed at pseudo-LTAs, blames the concept rather than her poor selection process. Rather than re-examine her approach to relationships, she opts to live alone.

Singles should be aware of the potential hazards of pseudo-LTAs. Adding a toothbrush to a man's or woman's residence does not constitute a commitment. For those men and women who are scared to be alone or unable to muster enough inner strength to carefully select the right long-term partner, pseudo-LTAs may be the closest to intimacy they ever get. One never-married man of forty-five was as disturbed at the breakup of his intermittent live-in relationship of three years as I have seen others to be after the dissolution of a seven-year marriage. He lives in Connecticut; his girlfriend lives in Manhattan. Three times a week, she slept over at his house. "Maybe it would have been better if we had been married," he told me. "Then at least we would have had the legal hassles to talk about. But this way, she just walked out of my life and we didn't have to make any further contact." Divorced persons I have interviewed, however, did not agree that fighting over property had a therapeutic effect; they felt it was a supremely destructive note on which to end a relationship. The Connecticut man's comments about the trauma of the breakup of even his intermittent live-in relationship emphasized to me that it is not the legal nature of the relationship that often determines how one handles its termination, but the meaning that the relationship had for each of its participants, and the expectations each had brought to it.

Trial marriages are the most acceptable form of LTA to singles. If, following a satisfactory trial marriage, a couple decides to legalize the relationship, they believe there is a very good chance that the marriage will succeed.

Many singles below the age of twenty-five believe in "trial marriage" because it seems the "thing to do." As one eighteen-year-old said, "I'd like to live with a man, and see if I would want to marry him. Someone I could have sex with, whenever I wanted to. Someone to talk to everyday." Upon further questioning, I discovered that she was frightened of making a mistake and marrying the wrong person. Trial marriage, she fantasized, would "guarantee" marital success.

Men and women who are fearful of marriage are more comfortable with the thought, or practice, of living with a member of the opposite sex in a "trial run." This I found to be especially true for divorced men and women who have good reason to be cautious before making another legal commitment. Paul, who proposed to his first wife after just ten dates, lived with his second wife for almost two years before they married. "My own experience," Paul explains, "has been that living together before marriage makes much sense and should be widely adopted." Miriam is a twenty-eight-year-old divorced college professor; she has been living with a man for the past four years. Although cohabitation is more acceptable now than fifteen years ago, Miriam believes it is still unconventional. "I get paranoid when we look for an apartment," Miriam explains. "What will the landlord think? Also my department chairman doesn't yet know that I have a male companion. What can I tell him?" Miriam is fortunate in that her family accepts her live-in arrangement, but she has to contend with the outside world, which she doesn't think is ready to understand her life-style.

Others cited fear of parental objections as the principal reason for avoiding cohabitation, even as a prelude to marriage. Sy, a twenty-one-year-old college student, is undecided about the subject of living together. "I'm probably in favor of it. It's like a trial run. But I worry about hurting other people. I respect my parents and I'm careful what I do so as not to make them terribly ashamed of me and find myself banished from the house." Elderly widows and widowers cite fear of invoking the shame of their children as a reason for their hesitation to live with a companion, although many reported they had simply neglected to clarify whether their lodger was also their sexual partner.

The idea of trial marriage is certainly not new; primitive cultures have used it for centuries. The Ifugaos of the Northern Philippines, for example, have a custom that is similar to the cohabitation arrangement in America today. R. F. Barton, who lived with the Ifugaos in the early 1900s and wrote about their customs, described how two or three trial marriages are generally necessary before a young man or woman selects a more permanent mate. Unmarrieds live in dormitories where sexual intercourse is permitted. Trial marriage is usually for those who have little or no property, who have been widowed, or who have dissolved an unsatisfactory contract marriage. (A contract marriage is usually made between the Ifugao children who will inherit a great deal of property. It is used to prevent a child from marrying "beneath his status," while in the common dormitory.)

Many trial marriages give both parties a chance to decide, without legal ramifications, whether marriage is a good idea. Carl is a computer programmer who is thirty-two years old; he is separated from his wife. His marriage, which lasted two years, was childless. Six months after he and his wife separated, he met Ann, with whom he lived in a shared household for over four years. Two months ago, they broke up. "We just realized that we had too many problems that could never be resolved," Carl explained. "We decided in a very rational way that we should not get married. It's really hard to be rational with someone with whom you've been living for four years, but this breakup is very different from the one with my wife. Ann and I still talk to each other on the phone; I think that I've spoken to my wife not more than three times in the past four years and it has always been about legal matters regarding the divorce." How does Carl find being single, the second time around? "It has been hard because my married friends don't want to be around me anymore. I think their wives are threatened by my singleness. They probably think I'm having all this sex and that their husbands will begin to get ideas. Otherwise, it hasn't been too bad. I'm actually enjoying it, though I don't think the enjoyment will last. In about six months to a year I think I'll be ready to settle down again. Still, I've discovered that I can do things for myself. Ann was so neat, I was afraid the apartment would turn into a pig pen after she left. Now I find that after I use a dish, I wash it."

Bob, who is a thirty-two-year-old divorced salesman, has been living with his girlfriend, Alice, a twenty-seven-year-old never-married woman, in a trial marriage for the last two years. Alice and Bob work at the same company. They became friends, gradually started a relationship, and drifted into living together. After sharing the same eight-by-ten studio apartment, they bought a house together and moved out to Long Island. They are planning to marry in a few months because they want to start a family. Alice, who "would have married Bob in a minute if he had asked me," went along with the living-together arrangement basically because of Bob's fears of relationships, fears generated by his first, unsuccessful marriage. "I would definitely not marry my ex-wife again," Bob explains, "because it was a tragic, immature mistake. But I'm marrying Alice, my best friend, in October." Alice, however, is afraid that what Bob has told her marriage is like will come true when they legalize their relationship. "Bob says that when people marry, they lose their independence and become dependent on each other. I hope that doesn't happen to us."

Alice's fear is a legitimate one; some cohabitating couples do not make successful marriage partners. A curious transformation occurs after the wedding ceremony. Whereas they had previously been able to establish their own rules, suddenly they find themselves comparing their situation to traditional marriage. A woman who did not mind paying half the rent when she was living with a man suddenly demands that her husband support her. Since he believed everything would stay the same—even after marriage—he refuses to comply with her new definitions. A couple who had worked out an individualized way of accepting or refusing social or family invitations now find that they are expected to go to business and family functions together. What was once a private relationship has now come under public scrutiny and in-laws, cousins, aunts, and uncles often pressure the newly-wed couple in totally unexpected ways. A weak relationship may buckle under traditional role requirements. An awareness of the possible drawbacks of marriage may, indeed, influence a couple to see their trial marriage as an alternative relationship. "I used to think that we were living together only to see if we might someday marry," Jane explained, "but just in the last week I've decided I don't want to get married. I like the way things are. I'll be honest with you. If I married John, I'd lose my five hundred dollars a month from social security [Jane is a widow]. And John just couldn't make up the difference. It's hard for my friends to accept that we may just continue to live together—and never marry. But I'm afraid if we married, everything would fall apart."

The problems faced by live-ins are frequently as awesome as the problems of married couples, and counselors for unwed couples have emerged in response to the specific needs of the cohabiting population. University of Iowa staff psychologist Richard Yates notes one of the principal differences in the problems of his living-together clients and those of his married ones: "If half of a living-together arrangement wants to get married, and the other half does not, a conflict arises over the depth of the partners' commitment to the relationship. This problem does not arise in a marriage; the commitment is understood. Both troubled couples may arrive at the same point—separation—but the processes will be different. Of course this is a generalization, but the living-together partner is less likely to work hard at resolving problems. Since there is usually a longer history, and a greater commitment, to a marital relationship, and the lives of the two are more intertwined—through shared friends and combined finances—the married couple has more at stake in salvaging the union."

Many living-together partners are as frightened as are marrieds of the possible failure of their relationship. Those who live together constantly reassess the nature of their relationship. Most of the live-ins that I interviewed had sustained their relationship over one or two years. Both people usually had full-time jobs. Those who did not want children found cohabitation more satisfactory than marriage, but once pregnancy was involved, a legal bond usually followed.

I interviewed Pearl, who lived with a man for five years, bore him a daughter, married him, and was divorced eight months later. "He was a child," Pearl explains. "He lived for today. He refused to save for a house. It was one thing when we were living together, but he got even worse after we married." Marilyn, who is twenty-four and lives in Hawaii, found the opposite to be true. "My husband and I lived together for ten months before we married in 1977. From the very start our relationship was open, honest, and serious. We settled right down to getting to know and love each other." Peggy has tried both pseudo-LTAs and a trial marriage since her divorce. "My thinking has changed," she told me. "I would rather date someone for a year or two and, if we're happy and the best of friends, then get married. If I have a trial marriage, I can't legitimately date others as a means of comparison. I'd rather take my time, be sure it's the real thing, and get married. Now I see trial marriages as the worst of both worlds—none of the rights or status of marriage, but none of the fun and freedom of dating."

If a trial marriage is going well, marriage will not ruin it. But if there are weaknesses, the extra burden of marriage—and the complicated expectations of parents, in-laws, friends, and employers—will probably erode the relationship. If marriage is used as a way of "saving" the LTA, it will have as little positive benefit as having a child does for a floundering marriage. "If we hadn't married, we would have broken up in another year," says a once-married woman who was married for five years. She and her ex-husband lived together for five months before they married. "We lived together for the wrong reasons and we married for the wrong reasons as well. Yet I know that if we hadn't married—and had the extra pressures of not wanting publicly to admit our failure—the relationship would have terminated a lot sooner, and with a lot less pain and financial hardship."

Barbara got her first apartment when she was nineteen years old, and found she was terrified of living alone. "Looking back I now realize that it was my inability to tolerate being alone that led to my instant involvement with John," she explained. "It all happened so quickly. We hardly knew each other. That 'instant' intimacy cost me four years of my life—we went from an intensified sexual/dating situation to living together for a few months to an ill-fated marriage."

The Living-Together Arrangements which I call alternatives to marriage are not casual or experimental relationships. Like most marriages, they do not sanction extra-marital sex. In fact, couples in this type of relationship tend to have higher standards of fidelity than many marrieds. They are setting their own rules, and therefore are far more diligent about following them. A forty-two-year-old divorced woman with two children recently moved in with an older divorced man whom she has been seeing for almost two years. She is amazed that even though she and her boyfriend agreed that either one could have affairs outside their relationship, neither has wanted to. "I don't see our relationship as a step toward marriage," she explained. "I see it as an alternative to marriage. We consider ourselves in a marital type of relationship, but with openness in terms of our sexual arrangement. We have agreed that we can see other people, if we choose to, but I haven't chosen to for the last few months—which is really strange.

"We have these discussions till four or five in the morning. My boyfriend says, 'I don't want us to sound like we're married. I don't want us to get into the rut of a "marital relationship." If I wanted that, I'd be married.' The good thing about our arrangement is that it leaves the door open; we have the option if we ever decide to exercise it. If we didn't have that kind of openness, we could not exist. It just would not have worked."

The increased social acceptance of alternatives to marriage is a blessing for those once-marrieds who are cynical about legal relationships. At least an alternative relationship offers intimacy and partial commitment. Some women who believe that an alternative to marriage is all that they want are surprised to find that they panic when parenting is not even considered by their partner. "I lived with him for eight years," a forty-year-old woman told me. "I wanted to get married and have children, but he liked the way things were." He found a younger woman, with whom he is now living, and she is living alone and trying to find a husband.

George and Mildred have lived together, and have been completely faithful to each other, for over fifteen years. They do not have any children, and do not want any. They live on their separate incomes, each paying part of the rent. Does Mildred consider herself married or single? "I consider myself single," Mildred told me. Legally, George and Mildred are single, but their profiles do not match those of the never-married men and women who live alone. They do not completely mirror the profiles of married couples either. Cohabiting couples tend to have more individualized relationships than their married counterparts. They tend to engage in more activities independent of their live-in companion and have less in-law contact. George and Mildred, for example, never go together to their respective parents for the Christmas holidays. Each one goes alone to his or her family. Mildred went through a mid-thirties crisis over whether or not she wanted to have a child. Since George is a struggling novelist, and has little money, she decided that they could not afford a child on her salary and resigned herself to childlessness. Victor and Robin have been living together for five years. Victor never married; Robin is divorced. "Occasionally I see Robin in the evenings," Victor says, "but she's so busy with her job, we just don't seem to have that much time together." Does he mind? "We're happy," Victor continued. "We both like what we're doing." So far, Robin confided, they have not had any discussions about whether or not to have children. Robin is thirty-four; Victor is thirty-six.

Marvin is a thirty-year-old never-married Ph.D. candidate in psychology who lives, and attends school, in Minneapolis. He and his girlfriend share a home. "I would say my relationship with Carol is the same as marriage," says Marvin. "When I was living with my first girlfriend, I always had a separate apartment where I could go if I wanted to." Will he marry Carol? Marvin laughed. "I doubt it. July second I met someone who was here for the summer. I was seeing her on the side. She just went back to Providence. It would really have wrecked my relationship with Carol if I had told her I was seeing someone else. I don't think I want to marry anyone yet."

Trudy and Tom have been living together for three years. Trudy, who is thirty-five, is divorced, as is forty-five-year-old Tom. "This is the happiest and closest Tom has been to a woman," Trudy, a writer, explains. "He never knew that a female could be a friend and a buddy, just like a man." Will they marry? Trudy visibly trembled when I said the word *marry*. "We're both scared. I don't feel ready for it yet, but then I might never feel ready for it. Tom wants me to be pregnant when we get married. We fantasize a lot about having a child, but I'm still working through the career-housewife dilemma. I've been in therapy for five months and Tom is even jealous of that relationship. I'm afraid of finding out whether or not he could handle the competition that a baby would add." Tom, who is a psychologist, works hard at their living-together arrangement, Trudy assures me. "We both feel that this is our last chance. If we can't work it out, we both lose, and neither of us can afford to lose another time."

Those who have suffered the failures of a marriage may be psychologically and financially unable to deal with the prospect of another divorce and hence opt for an alternative relationship to marriage. "I already have a family," a thirty-eight-year-old divorced anthropologist explains, "so I wouldn't get married to start another one. But I would live with a woman if I found someone with whom I wanted to share my life." Generally, long-term cohabiting couples agree to remain childless or already have children from previous marriages. When a married woman with children reports to me, "We just as easily could have lived together as be married," it indicates to me a wish to appear "with it" rather than a sincere consideration of the alternative.

**129**

The increase in the number of living-together arrangements that are alternatives to marriage has led to some innovative variations on such traditional concepts as wedding announcements. Thirty-nine-year-old Sara set up a household with her boyfriend, who is separated from his wife. A few months ago, they sent out printed announcements declaring that they were living together and that, on weekends, his four children would be staying with them. Sara has the difficult task of being a permanent live-in step-friend. As confusing as is the role of step-parent, that of a live-in man or woman is even more bewildering. On weekends, when her boyfriend's four children stay with them, Sara has to be an instant something. Parent? Friend? "I came out of the shower last weekend, dripping wet, and there was Sam with his nine-year-old son, lying on the bed, talking. I wanted to tell his son to 'get off my bed,' but they were having a nice father-and-son talk. We have two completely different households—one during the week and one on weekends." Sara, who has never married and has always lived alone, finds herself suddenly dealing with many instant situations—instant pseudo-marriage and instant-mother.

What legal rights do live-ins have? Practically none, presuming common-law marriage* is not in effect. Ac-

* In the following states—Alabama, Colorado, Florida, Georgia, Idaho, Iowa, Kansas, Michigan, Mississippi, Montana, Ohio, Oklahoma, Pennsylvania, Rhode Island, South Carolina, South Dakota, and Texas—as long as a couple maintain residency for the required cohabitation time and they have evidence that they have declared themselves as "Mr. and Mrs.," such as a joint bank account or credit card, their liaison is termed a common-law marriage and is considered as valid as a formal marriage, and can be terminated only by death or divorce.

cording to Adriane G. Berg, an expert in marital law and a New York attorney, "Most states are very clear in denying any property rights to live-ins as a way of discouraging this type of arrangement." Marriage, it is still believed, is in the best interest of the family, and the state. Gloria, a divorced New York woman in her middle forties, lived in an arrangement with all the characteristics of marriage except the legal piece of paper, for four years. Brian, her cohabitant, who was also divorced, died suddenly, at the age of forty-five, of a heart attack. For the first time in her adult life (she went directly from her first marriage to living with Brian, whom she had met while she was still married) Gloria is now alone, and has to support herself. I spoke with Gloria just five weeks after Brian's death. She was in the stage of bereavement where her anger at Brian was surfacing; she was also scared by her financial vulnerability. Even though she had contributed to the purchase of the apartment's furniture, Brian had used his personal checks. Therefore, proof of ownership was in Brian's name. His ex-wife was suing his estate for back alimony and back child support. "It's ironic," Gloria said in our interview, "they hated each other with a vengeance when he was alive. Now, she may be the one to profit from his death." About a year before his death, Brian had taken out an insurance policy, with Gloria as his beneficiary. She would be getting $10,000 from that, but she was afraid that someone was going to take away all of the furniture because it was part of the estate of the deceased. Another woman, who has been living with someone for more than ten years, pointed out to me a legal limitation because of cohabitation. "If he needed an operation," she said, "I couldn't even sign for it."

In those states that do not recognize common-law marriage there are six key legal rights not guaranteed to those who live together. These rights are in the areas of inheritance, sex, property, intrafamily offenses, taxes, and marital duties.* A surviving spouse in almost every state has the right to part of the deceased spouse's estate; unless a joint or mutual will is made, a couple living together do not have a right to each other's property in the event of death. Sex is considered a right in marriage; proof that that right has been denied is grounds for divorce—*constructive abandonment.* As regards property, a lawyer told me of an interesting case in which the family of a woman who was killed in an airplane crash had sued the estate of her live-in boyfriend, who was also killed. Since the couple had not made a joint will, a year after the couple's death, the claim was denied. In some states, intrafamily offenses are settled in family or criminal court; parties who are not legally married would have to take charges of aggravated assault to criminal court. The major advantage of cohabitation is that where the partners' incomes are similar, taxes tend to be lower when separate returns are filed. "I always get a refund," a woman who has lived with her boyfriend for more than a decade explains. "My married friends who are making the same income but file jointly seem to pay two or three thousand dollars *to* the government." Marital duties are those functions of each partner that are assumed to be a "right" (taking care of the home, supporting the fam-

* To some extent, *Marvin v. Marvin* and its ramifications may modify these statements.

ily), although these "rights" are being questioned as the roles for men and women in the society are being reevaluated and redefined.

With the assistance of a good attorney it is possible to gain many assurances for the live-in. For example, if live-ins make sure that their real property is held in joint tenancy, they will be able to own it in much the same way as if married (which means that if one dies, the other has the right of survivorship). Couples can make a will or take out insurance to provide death benefits. The duration of the relationship obviously determines whether such questions are even raised.

In any kind of LTA, it is crucial that both partners be clear about their goals. It is all too easy to dismiss emotional difficulties in a "temporary" relationship, but for a small portion of the living-together population, the breakup of a relationship of even only short duration will produce intense feelings of rejection, and the sufferer will not have recourse to the social or professional supports available to the divorced or widowed. Yet I am convinced that all forms of LTAs will continue to increase in the next decade as more and more Americans search for their personal solutions to the need for intimacy and the fear of legal commitment.

# 7

→>>→>>→>>

# Taking the Good With the Bad:
# The Consequences of Singleness

Committed singles create for themselves a relatively stable life-style not unlike that of their married counterparts. Those who view their singleness as transitional show no such permanence in the way they live. There is the implicit understanding and expectation that major changes in life-style will occur when they become intimately involved with another person. This period of marking time seems to me to be both wasteful and somewhat self-defeating. Nevertheless, some singles do "get it together." I was interested to find out what makes for a happy single.

Some basic characteristics are common to happy singles. They generally have self-esteem, and consequently feel desirable. They are people who *would* belong to a club that would have them as members. They tend to seek and find fulfillment in life, the most common route being through a career. As a rule, the happy single takes his or her work seriously and enjoys it. Fulfillment is also achieved through friends, hobbies, cultural activities, charitable work, physical exercise (for self-improvement and as a social outlet) and romantic involvements—if and when they occur. The happy single enjoys life, and seeks someone to enjoy it with, while the unhappy single wants someone to *make* him or her happy.

Greg is one of the happy singles that I interviewed. I was impressed by his positive self-image and his assertiveness. "On the whole, I'm pleased with my life," Greg, in his late twenties, told me, "although I'd like to be rich and famous, of course." Greg accepts his singleness as a fact of life; up till now, he has not yet met the right one. "I have never been engaged," he told me, "nor have I ever lived with a woman. I just haven't wanted to—so far. I do fool around, however." In addition to the usual "search" ("I'm not afraid to ask a woman out, go on a date, and see what develops"), Greg is an officer and attends regular meetings of his local chapter of the Junior Chamber of Commerce (Jaycees). Once a month, he and fifteen colleagues meet and, over dinner, they discuss physics. Greg has known his best friend, Craig, since high school. He and Craig play squash occasionally and, alone or with a date, Greg also has dinner with Craig and his wife, Joan, who is an excellent cook. Greg has become friendly with Joan and, in many ways, his relationship with a happily married couple is representative of the kind of stable relationships happy singles have. Greg is not hunting for a wife, but he has his eyes wide open in case she does come along. He's not in a rush for marriage, but with that "certain someone" he looks forward to it as his next step. Greg does not "blame" fate, or himself, for his singleness.

A happy single, I discovered, is quite different from someone who is on a post-separation "high." The latter's burst of enthusiasm for the "free, single life" is more a negative reaction to an unsatisfactory relationship than a positive reaction to the benefits of singleness. Indeed, the person who is suddenly single, who initially proclaims the merits of an unattached life, often becomes the disenchanted single who can see only drawbacks to the single life-style.

Satisfied singles *relate* to others; disgruntled ones *cling* to others. Donna is a separated single whose euphoria quickly dissipated. Thirty-two-years old, divorced, and the mother of a seven-year-old son, Donna feels basically unhappy with herself. She needs men to fill in her free time and bolster her self-image. "I'm dating six men right now," she recently told me, "so when any one relationship breaks up, I'm not despondent. This is the happiest I've ever been."

The contented single neither credits nor faults singleness for his or her pleasures or problems. He or she simply *is* single—for better and worse. That role, like the marital one, requires certain adjustments. If married couples must strive to improve their ability to communicate and compromise, the contented unattached single has learned that he or she must strive to stay vital, enjoy limited "at home" time alone, and develop a variety of friends who will help provide some of the human contact that married people have with each other.

"A completely busy life" is the phrase most contented singles repeated to me. (But not so busy that there's no time if someone special does come along.) A chef in his fifties, who lives alone, has music as his constant companion, and also gives dinner parties almost every night of the week. A lawyer in his early thirties, who discovers his parents are planning to be away for Thanksgiving, takes a vacation in Europe instead of feeling sorry for himself because he is alone. The key to the successful life of the contented unattached single is people. Not necessarily romantic involvements (though they help) but straightforward contact with people.

Optimistic unattached singles also mix their friends, so that they are included in the social activities of married couples as well as other singles. A single in her late thirties, who is a schoolteacher, believes the diversity and range of her long-standing friendships have kept her sane. It has also provided a much-needed stability to her life over the past twenty years, as romantic involvements have pulled and tugged.

I discovered that contented singles, because they are people and activity oriented, are naturally "visible" and are receptive to potential friendships or romantic relationships. They rarely need to rely on "singles-oriented" activities. A twenty-five-year-old midwestern Chicano woman summed up why she felt such forced "meeting people" activities were counterproductive: "Anyone I would meet by hanging out in a singles bar or joining a church group wouldn't really have a chance, because the very way that we met would have been dishonest. I'm a lot more likely to meet somebody interesting on a weekend bike trip, because I like doing that and presumably he's out there because he likes doing it too. I'm just going to continue doing what I enjoy doing, and keep my eyes open." Her attitude is similar to that of older widows and widowers who accept the single-ness that follows the death of a spouse. They do not compare their single life to their former married life. One is the past; the other the present. If their emotional and sexual needs predispose them to a second marriage, they will make an effort—but not a desperate one—to find someone with whom to stroll up the aisle.

The happy single sees his or her premarital life as viable and important. Experiences count even if they are not shared. As one contented single put it: "After five years, I'm still looking, but I'm not discouraged. I know how much I've improved in the last five years, and I'm sure my Miss Right has spent the last five years getting better and better as well."

Behind a contented unattached single person is an elaborate network of friends, activities, and romantic relationships. A woman of thirty-three, who has never married, babysits for a young married couple who live close by. She does not accept any money; she does it to fulfill her need to be around, and involved with, chil-dren. The single discovers that it is unnecessary to deny himself or herself an experience because an escort is unavailable. Contented singles are comfortable being alone—in their homes or outside. They are not afraid to eat out alone, go to the movies alone on a Saturday "date" night, travel to another state or country, or go to a dinner party even if their presence will mean an uneven number of guests. Same-sex friends are not abandoned—or appointments cancelled—because a ro-mantic prospect suddenly appears.

Contented singles do not debase themselves by en-tering into relationships just to "get through the night." They will not let fear of loneliness put them into a potentially compromising situation. They put their own needs first but are not so self-centered that the needs or wishes of others are not considered. If divorced, their bitterness toward their ex-spouses has been replaced by a tempered reappraisal of the past. If never married, they are able to put prior romances in perspective. These contented singles are as sure about what they do *not* want as they are about what they want. They will not allow their singleness to be an excuse for settling for second best. "I don't want to be accountable to anyone but myself," one single woman of thirty told me. "I don't want to be self-conscious about what I say or how I look. I don't want to feel nervous in someone else's presence. I don't want to listen to someone else's one-note songs. I'd rather be alone." For her, singleness produces less anxiety than intimacy. For others like her, living alone is better than living with "the wrong one."

Some marrieds that I met refused to believe that there *are* cheerful singles. They could envision only a stereotype of the suffering, desolate single (much as other marrieds that I met needed to believe that singles prefer being unattached to being with someone). One married man, who lives in a suburban bedroom community, said to me, "As a married man, I'd be very happy to find out what a terrible life single people have." He might have been enlightened by what a California psychologist, who is single, had to say to me on the subject. "A permanent relationship is not necessarily a more satisfactory one," he began. "I know some people who get married, and stay married, who are no more or less happy than those who stay single. Even if someone is uninvolved with a member of the opposite

sex, he or she may be happier than the person who set-
tles for any relationship just to avoid being alone."

The incidence of singleness will vary according to the
size of the community in which a single man or woman
lives. I spoke with one single man who moved from a
rural upstate New York community to a larger city because he found the rural setting socially difficult. "Everyone knew everyone else," Marvin, who is thirty-seven,
explains. "If you walked into town with a woman, everyone knew about it. I moved out of town, and had a
house set off in the woods, so that my guests could
come and go as they pleased. But the most striking part
of being single in a rural area is that there's nothing
to do. There are no organizations to join. Everything
is on a small scale. There's no such thing as privacy.
In winter—which lasted most of the year—it's difficult to
go anywhere. A friend of mine was willing to drive up
to Syracuse for dates, but I found that kind of driving
too much for a weekend. If you want to be alone, a
rural area would attract you. But if you want to stay
single, and have a social life, it's a lot harder. There are
just fewer women to choose from."

Now that Marvin has moved to a larger city in
Pennsylvania, he is content with his social life. For the
time being he does not want to marry and he needs a
wide selection of women to supply him with steady
dates. "Most of the women who grew up here have
either married or moved away, but a number of profes-
sionals have come here. I'd like to move back to New
York . . . if I could find the kind of job I have here.
It's easiest to be single there."

One often-cited advantage of being single in a rural

area is the possibility it offers of forming close friendships. Wayne, a professional man in his late twenties,
lives alone in a four-bedroom home that he recently
purchased. He frequently socializes—and has become
good friends—with his employees and their spouses.
Marvin also found that he had made close to twenty
friends in less than two years.

Does a particular type of community foster singleness? Do those with a "single type" personality gravi-
tate toward settings that provide fewer social opportunities? Wayne, who is only one hour from Boston and
one hour from Cape Cod, does not find the limited
choices of women in his small town a problem. For now,
he's content to work hard at his job and his hobbies—
painting, cooking, and gardening. But as a friend of
Wayne's explained to me, even when Wayne attended
graduate school in Boston he was not particularly active socially. Ultimately, if one is so inclined, one can
"stay" single—or alone—in San Francisco as easily as
one can in Mason City, Illinois.

For a small portion of the population, singleness will
always be the chosen way of life. "I've been single for
the last five years, and I've managed well," a divorced
woman with two children, ages ten and twelve, told me.
She is currently living with a man whom she dated for
almost two years and finds life wonderful. "I know a
lot of single people here in Virginia who are quite
happy with their life-style. I know one guy who doesn't
want a close relationship with a woman. He wouldn't
know what the hell to do with it. The idea frightens
him. So he has a number of friends, and a number of
sexual liaisons. He has his work and he's, quote, happy,

**141**

unquote. I think the single life-style is something this kind of person can now have without feeling like a misfit."

Are there physical consequences to remaining single? Compared to marrieds, singles (never-married, once-married, and widowed) smoke more, drink more, visit physicians more often, have more car accidents, and have greater incidences of cancer of the digestive system. There are also sexual consequences to being single without a steady love relationship. The hazards of instant intimacy—sexual activity that is not matched by emotional commitment—have led the majority of singles that I interviewed to abandon the practice of one-night stands. "I've been celibate for the past four months," a thirty-year-old divorced woman, who moved to London from Manhattan a year ago, wrote to me. "I went through a promiscuous phase the year after my separation and I just broke up with someone with whom I lived for the past year. Now I want to remarry." Some singles fantasize about instant sex. "I would like to have a horny man living across the hall, who would be available on five minutes' notice," a woman of twenty-nine told me. "I've gone out with this man five times," another woman of the same age complained, "and he hasn't so much as touched the button on my blouse."

For many singles, the drive to find someone for a long-term relationship is at cross-purposes with the need for immediate sexual and emotional closeness. "The men can just smell how desperate she is," a twenty-three-year-old woman told me about her girl-friend. "She wants to get married so badly that she can't even think about anything else anymore. She doesn't even smile when she meets someone new."

Time and again, married women would say, "Out of my five closest girlfriends, I was the one who least wanted to marry and I was the one to marry first. I can't understand it. Of the ones who really wanted to marry, well, two are still single—ten years later."

The frequency with which singles have sex varies enormously, from a man in his late twenties who has it "three or more times every week" to a divorced woman in her mid-fifties who never has sex and "does not miss it." The frequency with which singles have sexual relations has more to do with their attitude and opportunities than with their age. Thus, a never-married woman in her mid-twenties, who dates regularly but rarely feels a relationship merits sexual intimacy, reports fewer sexual experiences than a divorced woman of forty-eight who approves of sex on a first date and as a way of initiating new relationships.

One of the myths about singles is that, for them, singleness and sex are synonymous. For the majority of singles, however, I discovered that lack of sexual intimacy was a chronic complaint. I rarely found that unattached singles over thirty-five who live alone have overactive sex lives, even though they do often have active lives in other areas—committee meetings, dinners out with friends (male or female), night classes, and so forth. A typical response from men and woman to my question as to the frequency of sex was "once a month" or "when I meet someone I care about—once or twice a year." Rare was the reply "fourteen times a week," which I received from an actress who is dating seven men. The majority of single men and women have far less sex than is thought. Why? "Sleeping around," as one twenty-six-year-old woman termed it, is still condemned by society and by the singles themselves. "Most men think because you are single and live alone, you 'screw' around," a midwestern radio interviewer explained. "Because I don't, it can be discouraging. The guys say, 'Well, what's wrong with you?' " A woman of thirty-four found that when she ceased being sexually available, the number of her dates dwindled. "I let it be known that I was 'liberated.' It worked. Men asked me out. They can sense it. I don't attribute not having dates anymore to where I live. It's me. I'm almost positive it's me." Single men are questioning too much sex and not enough loving with the "wrong" partner just as much as are single women. "I never thought I'd say this," a man of forty-four explains, "but if I don't feel something for a woman, no matter how attractive she is, I don't want to have sex with her. I find sex boring unless there's a strong emotional bond. I used to want sex every night, with almost anyone who'd want me." "I find that sex without love now seems perfunctory," a thirty-year-old man says. "I'm so eager for love, and so disenchanted with sex, that I can go months without sex and not even feel horny. Am I growing up, or just getting old?"

Singles who had sexual relations only once or twice a year were able to share with me their observations of certain behavior patterns in themselves—fidgetiness, nervousness, insomnia, lethargy, compulsive eating—which they felt were directly related to their deprivation. Most startling were the complaints from singles who had divorced because the sexual aspects of their marriage were unsatisfactory. After the frantic phase of somewhat indiscriminate sexual activity had tapered off, and they were reserving sexual intimacy for those they felt an emotional closeness with as well, they found that they had no sex at all. "Even though my husband and I did it only once a month," a young divorced woman told me, "I laugh now at how I complained about that meager pattern. It has been so long since I've had sex with anyone. I just hope it's like riding a bicycle —that I'll remember how when I finally meet someone with whom I want to take a spin around the park."

Carol, who is just thirty, has had the same boyfriend for the past ten years, but she has also had seven short-term affairs. Carol dropped out of college after two years; she now works as a secretary. She grew up, and still lives, in New York City. Her on-again/off-again boyfriend does not live with her; they see each other about once a month. Even though her boyfriend still avoids discussing marriage, Carol is sure they will eventually marry and raise a family. "I was just twenty-one," Carol says, "when I had sex for the first time with my boyfriend. I've regretted having sex with the other seven men over the years because it didn't mean anything to them and it didn't mean anything to me. Yet I believe that if a woman can enjoy sex with many men before she's married, it doesn't hurt her relationship with her husband at all. It has given her experience and it's just as important for a woman today to have experience as it is for a man."

"I still think men have fantasies about wanting to marry a virgin," says Linda, a thirty-five-year-old never-married woman who grew up on a farm in California and now lives alone. "There are some men with whom, over the years, I've regretted having sex. I was not pressured about sex the way most women my age were. When I was eight, ten, twelve, thirteen, or whatever, my mother said, 'Linda, sleep with a man or live with him before you get married, but don't get married until you want to start a family.' So I wasn't brought up to be a virgin and by the time I was in college, I was having conflicts about my virginity. But now I realize that instant sexual intimacy creates an illusion of emotional intimacy. If you hop into bed right away, oftentimes, the more difficult part of the relationship never develops. But I'm too impatient to let sex come after I know someone. I used to wait until the fifth or sixth date, but since I passed thirty—maybe because I feel time is running out—I've had sex on the first or second date."

Maria, who is thirty-four, unlike Linda and Carol, is living with a man. She was married for three years and has been divorced since 1975. She lives with her current boyfriend of a year and a half in a luxury apartment on Manhattan's East Side; her boyfriend pays half the rent. Maria, a music therapist, grew up in a suburban community in Pennsylvania and is from a wealthy family. She says she has had sex with hundreds of men. "Although I think I had more experience than my ex-husband, we never really talked about it. I was faithful while we were married. The sexual revolution benefited me in that it gave me the knowledge really to do something about my sexual problems, but it was easier to fuck than to expose myself. I used sex to avoid relationships."

Says Carol: "In my case, the sexual revolution worked against me. It brought about the reform in the abortion laws. It has become easier to get an abortion than to roll off a log. I terminated a four-month pregnancy three years ago. But years back, my boyfriend and I would have gotten married and we would have had our child, maybe another one by now, and my boyfriend would have had to shape up and become a little bit more responsible. The sexual revolution made it easier for him, and others, to get out of relationships. People are looser now. Men *and* women, not just women. Less responsibility, fewer long-term commitments."

A divorced man who lives with his parents disagrees. At thirty-one, he finds that women have expected him to make a pass on the first date. He would have preferred to wait. Men and women are confused about what is "right," "contemporary," "healthy," and "natural" when it comes to sex. Living by one's own standards is more demanding than living by those of society.

If one lacks the opportunity for daily intimacy, what are the possible psychological consequences? Dr. Anne B. Somers analyzed national health statistics that substantiated that, in 1975, singles had a higher number of admissions to psychiatric hospitals than a comparable married population:

| Marital Status | Number of Psychiatric Hospital Admissions Per 100,000 Persons |
|---|---|
| Marrieds | 90 |
| Never-marrieds | 685 |
| Widowed | 701 |
| Separated/Divorced | 865 |

I interviewed a twenty-four-year-old man who moved back with his parents because he found the "silence" of singleness too stressful. "I lived alone for a year after college," he explains, "but coming home from work with no one to talk to till the next day frightened me."

Singles who live alone report overuse of television as a substitute for someone to talk to as well as heavy phone use in the evenings to compensate for the lack of a flesh-and-blood contact.

Loneliness is the most often cited consequence of singleness. The everyday existence of the single who lives alone contains the same emotional traps as were faced by prisoners of war who were isolated for long periods of time. As Lt. Colonel Richard A. Levy and Major Jesse L. Green reported in their paper on Vietnam POWs, "The solo inmate spent much of his time attempting to communicate with his fellows." Since the guards "harshly discouraged" communication efforts of the POWs, once contact was made with a fellow prisoner "a laborious exchange of information would take place (one letter at a time) followed by recapitulation and sharing of a lifetime of experiences." Singles who have been single too long similarly pounce on new contacts in an effort to fill in the long tract of time in which there has been no social contact. One fifty-nine-year-old divorced man was so overwhelmed by the lively conversation he had with a single woman whom he took to dinner that he commented, "My throat was dry." They had not stopped talking for five hours. A single woman on a weekend trip found that Monday morning she had laryngitis because of the nonstop conversations she had engaged in since the previous Friday night. It is not uncommon for singles who live alone to go from five in the evening till the next morning at work without face-to-face contact with anyone.

The way that singles try to fill up their free time mirrors Levy and Green's description of what the POWs did to get through their captivity: "physical exercise (as much as six hours daily), educational programs, religious activities, withdrawal and fantasy, introspection, recall of the past, humor, pacing, sleep, planning escape, planning the future, personal hygiene, and games (checkers and cards)." Levy and Green found that, after release, the POWs expressed the need for the "periods of solitary" that they had experienced during their captivity. Those, however, who had been in solitary confinement for prolonged periods during captivity avoided "lonely motel rooms during business trips, frequently staying at the home of another POW." It would be interesting to study whether there is a significant difference between the marriages of those who have been single for a prolonged period and of those who have had just a few years of singleness. Perhaps a man or woman who experiences years of singleness can never relinquish a need for separateness and time alone.

Does marriage really cure loneliness? Generally, the time spent with a spouse, live-in lover, boyfriend, or girlfriend was cited by happy partners as the best part of the day. "I have my best friend—my wife—around all the time," writes a married man of forty-two who lives in the Midwest, "and I'm never alone inside." "When I was single," an advertising account executive of twenty-five told me, "I would get depressed and not have anyone to pull me out of it." "When I'm in love," a woman of forty-two who has never married says, "I'm never lonely and even my work goes better."

Some singles deal with their singleness by traveling. Anita, a sculptress in her early forties, has many married or younger friends and rarely lacks for companionship. Since she left her native New York, she has lived five years in London, two years in France, two years in Italy, four years in San Francisco, and one year in Laguna Beach, California. Instead of seeking to put down roots in one place, she likes to keep moving, collecting friends with whom she has active correspondence. When we last spoke, she was involved with an older man, but she was going to the West Coast for the summer—just as she seemed to have established a routine in New York. Anita does a lot of entertaining, surrounding herself with her friends, and has "garage sales" of her latest work. Melanie, a divorced woman who is a saleswoman for a computer company, spent the first five years of her post-marriage singleness traveling around the country. One year she was out of town, on and off, for eight months; her trips were intermittent, so she just about had time to unpack and repack. She is finally realizing that her excessive traveling has been a way to avoid new relationships—and the possibility of making another mistake in a second marriage. "I'm getting tired of traveling," she told me.

Numerous researchers have discovered that singles place a high premium on their jobs. My findings confirmed that, but I also discovered that the workaholism to which singles are prone often alternates with apathy toward work and poor performance. One single woman, for example, is overproductive Monday through Thursday; she can barely function on Fridays because of her pre-weekend blues. Numerous living-alone singles in their early thirties also describe a "burn-out" syndrome; their overly work-oriented twenties, without the reinforcement of emotional satisfaction, they feel, is directly related to their current lack of work incentive.

There is a relationship between prolonged singleness

and diminished self-respect. What are some of the dating patterns of insecure singles that provide insight into their low self-esteem? (1) Being excessively dominated by the person one is dating. An example of this is the man (or woman) who allows his girlfriend to cancel a date at the last minute even if it embarrasses or inconveniences him. He puts up with whatever she says or does and is unable to assert himself. (2) Accepting very late night phone calls from drunken boyfriends (or girlfriends), or last-minute invitations for a Saturday night out. The single with low self-esteem is afraid to express his or her need for respect for fear of "losing out" on a date. (3) "Buying" affection by showering gifts on uninterested dates. (4) Carrying on prolonged liaisons with married men or women, even if this means compromising deeper beliefs in fidelity and courtesy to the married partner's spouse.

To thrive emotionally, the single person must get out, meet people, and develop relationships, both of a romantic nature and otherwise. Although the single persons that I interviewed seemed to be divided into two camps—those who actively sought out social opportunities and those who felt they should leave possible romance to fate—I believe there is a need for singles to reexamine whether they are paying "psychological dues" to loneliness and isolation. Margaret, a thirty-four year-old woman with the "what comes along" approach, is overweight, depressed, frustrated, and socially backward for her years. Yet she refuses actively to seek out new friends—male or female. Her pride gets in the way of that seeming admission of personal needs.

In the school or college setting, where virtually everyone is single and eligible, it is easier for men and women to come together. They constantly bang into each other in the hallways and classes; they attend the same sports events; someone knows someone else who wants to introduce that boy to that girl. When that single population disperses and a large percentage of it marries, those who remain (or, later on, become) single find it much more difficult to locate their single peers.

Although singles bars, dating organizations, and singles apartment complexes are the most visible products of the growing singles industry, these are certainly not representative of all the avenues open to those unattached men and women who wish to meet new people. They exist for those persons who are unable, or unwilling, to find more personal solutions to their singleness. Those who frequent singles bars do so because they either like the atmosphere or have nowhere else to go. For many singles who have just broken off with someone, these bars provide a transition to a more individualized way of meeting new people. But, as the majority of singles pointed out to me, they could not feel comfortable frequenting a singles bar.

So what do singles do? Where can they go? From my total sampling, I discovered that the following means of meeting new people were listed, in order of decreasing frequency:

> *Most frequent*
> Through a friend
> At parties
> Through a hobby or interest
> Through school or work
> Talking to a stranger

*Less frequent*

Blind dates
Singles bars
Bars
Any kind of social or community function
Joining a health club
Answering, or placing, an ad

*Least frequent*

Professional introduction services
Video-dating services
Call girls or prostitutes
Singles resorts
Singles clubs

Although the singles industry may bring two people together, the evolution of their relationship is a purely individual matter. A management executive of thirty-one, who has never married, went on a singles weekend and enjoyed the sports activities and the chance to meet new people—women and men. "When people ask me how my weekend was," she explained, "I tell them, 'I met this terrific woman.' They all look at me as if I'm nuts. But I then tell them that making new women friends is as important to me now as meeting a man." "I went to a singles vacation package week in the Caribbean a few years ago," a thirty-two-year-old nutritionist told me. "I didn't meet a man, but I met lots of good people and I had a ball. I have some friends who are single who won't go anywhere alone. They just sit home all the time. Before I had a boyfriend, I used to go to bars alone. It felt good just to talk to people and to be able to go in alone without feeling intimidated."

**153**

When someone talks about the "singles scene," it is usually singles bars that are implied. There is a distinction between singles bars and neighborhood bars. The singles bars function primarily as meeting places for singles; drinking, eating, or listening to music are secondary considerations. Once a bar develops a reputation as a singles bar, it is difficult to walk in without the other customers assuming one is there primarily to socialize. Many singles, traveling in pairs, hop from one singles bar to another. I learned that word of mouth is still the best way to find a singles bar to match a particular individual's social standards. *How to Pick Up Girls*, a book based on interviews with twenty-five women, is initially offensive in its male chauvinist viewpoint ("The first thing a man looks for in a woman is good looks and sexiness. The first thing a woman looks for in a man is a good *personality*"), but my interviews with all but the most ardent feminists—from eighteen-year-old students to forty-year-old office workers to eighty-eight-year-old widows—tended to confirm author Eric Weber's statement that men look at a woman's physique as a prime consideration for "making a move." The women I interviewed admitted, however, that they, too, were initially attracted by physical appearance; personality was a secondary consideration. Talking to those who frequented singles bars, I concluded that if women adhere to the old-fashioned rules of waiting to be asked, and if both parties are careful in how they follow up on an initial contact, the bar scene can serve the same social function as the college mixer. In the last few years, some six thousand discos have been added to the number of singles bars as places to meet. A well-known dancing spot in New York City, a decades-old institution for meeting, eating, and socializing, has even added a disco. A woman who met her first husband there returned, thirty years later, after a successful twenty-three-year marriage ended by her husband's death, to find her new husband. A twenty-nine-year-old never-married man, however, said he would never set foot in there. "Don't ever mention that place to me," he shouted during an interview. He wasn't wild about orange juice or farina either.

Many singles who would never venture into a singles bar will frequent a neighborhood bar. A forty-year-old divorced woman who lives in Philadelphia told me, "I only go to one bar alone, where I know the owner and all the staff." In every community, bars develop reputations for providing a desirable atmosphere, good music, or good food. At some of these meeting places, whether you find a "new love" or not is of secondary importance; but you may meet a new same-sex friend or even get a producer for your play or a gallery owner to show your work. What singles who frequent any kind of bar assured me, over and over again, was that if you do not leave your sexual or personal mores at the bar door, this can be a viable way of meeting people.

The following two stories illustrate just how difficult it is to separate the reality and the fantasy of the bar scene. The first tale is from a thirty-four-year-old never-married woman who works for a major television network station in Manhattan. After work, on a Friday, she decided to go to a bar near her office. "They were packed three deep," she explains. "All the men had such hungry looks! I just walked out." The second tale is about a woman whose first husband of twenty-five years had recently died. She had never in her life gone into a bar, but some girlfriends convinced her to come along. One of the girlfriends explained: "That night she met Fred and they've been happily married ever since." Were all the men hungry at that first bar or were they just trying to find a way to meet someone when, sadly, too few options seemed available?

The growth of singleness has certainly stimulated the development of innovative mate-finding techniques. Many local and nationally distributed newspapers and magazines, such as the *New York Review of Books*, *The Nation*, the *Saturday Review*, the *Boston Phoenix*, and the *Village Voice*, publish personal ads written by those seeking dates or mates. Practically every type of situation is described—gays who need straight dates to take to business functions; fat women looking for men who appreciate Rubenesque females; elderly widows; young never-marrieds; widowers with children; divorced women searching for non-chauvinistic men; career women looking for equal males; old-fashioned women looking for husbands to support them, and so forth. Judi McMahon's persuasive article, "Sensational Female Seeks Male Equal for Serious Sharing," legitimized that method of mate hunting for many who previously would have rejected such a scheme. One widower with an M.B.A. read McMahon's article and placed two ads in the *Village Voice*—he received eighty responses, out of which he had twenty dates. One woman, who placed two ads searching for a mate, received forty responses—everything from store-bought cards to original designs to photocopied form replies to extensive typed resumés to two-page handwritten letters. Only one of the forty letters was offensive—from a man who detailed the size of his genital organ. It surprised her how much information many men provided on the basis of only a few lines in an advertisement. Those who signed their letters "Love" were immediately discarded. Those whose names were followed by numbers (indicating their incarceration in a prison) were also put aside. Offers to share an apartment, or travel together cross-country, were also ignored. She found that the greatest benefit of actually meeting twenty-some eligible singles in such a relatively short period of time was her reevaluation of her own priorities about the type of person with whom she might want to be involved. Instead of an imaginary checklist of attributes, she was face to face with numerous individuals who either did or did not appeal to her. "I had just broken up with someone with whom I had been seriously involved for six months," she told me. "I just didn't want to go back to my old method of trying to meet new people, namely, waiting around for the phone to ring. It had also been so long since I had had to 'small-talk' that I really learned a lot from having something like twenty 'first dates' within a two-week period." The ad method also provides those who are not instantly physically attractive—and might have a harder time "picking someone up"—with a chance to present themselves in a letter or a phone call. A forty-nine-year-old man, who had recently separated from his wife, told me that he found answering ads had proven a good way for him to ease back into the single world. He conceived of the meeting-someone-through-an-ad process as involving three stages: (1) finding in the reply to the ad something about the writer that makes her (him) worth pursuing, (2) being pleased enough by the initial phone contact to make a date, (3)

finding that the reality lives up to the fantasies generated by the letter and the telephone conversation. "I
find it is difficult to predict why someone gets from
stage one to stage two," he explained. "And there are
few that get to stage three."

Professional introduction services—such as computer
dating, videotape matchmakers, date-a-mate listings,
and matrimonial services—are another controversial
component of the singles industry. Journalist John Godwin "joined a total of fifty computer matching outfits,
lonely-hearts clubs, singles organizations, dating societies, swingers circles, escort agencies, matrimonial bu-
reaus, encounter groups, game rooms and correspondence services" and reported his results in *The Mating
Trade*. Godwin concludes that it is because crime has
become so rampant in America today—and men and
women are reluctant even to walk the streets by themselves let alone talk to strangers—that a mating trade
has had to develop "in an age and country of unsur-
passed communications." Although I empathize with
Godwin's awareness of how violent and dangerous
America is today, I think that fear of crime is not the
major reason for the professional introduction services.
Even more crucial is the cult of self that characterizes
American society: a "looking out for number one" mentality that leads the single person to seek the remedy
for his or her solitude through whatever means are
available. Perhaps businesses which thrive on making
matches will help where friends and relatives have often
failed.

Bob is a thirty-one-year-old schoolteacher who paid
a $250 fee to a matrimonial service for one year of un-
limited service. What that meant was that each month

he would be supplied with a minimum of three names of suitable women who had come to the marriage broker for similar services. Why did he do it? "When you're looking for Ms. Right," he said, "you can't afford to neglect any opportunities." Bob is pleasant looking, athletic, a good conversationalist, has two master's degrees, but is shy.

A young woman who registered with the same service was given a special rate of $35 for three names. Yet within three days, five names, addresses, and phone numbers arrived in the mail; a month later, for no additional charge, another three names and numbers were received. Only one of the eight men called, but she had the option of calling them. At first she would not call them, accepting what the wife of the marriage broker said to her: "The men that come to us are old-fashioned. They'll do the calling. They'll do the planning for the dates. They'll pick up the checks." When she did finally call one of the men who had failed to initiate contact, she learned that she was "geographically undesirable." She was, however, sufficiently pleased with the one man whom she did meet through the service that she went out with him a second time. That date proved to be the last one, however, and she began to wonder if all the trouble and expense was worth it. She also began to doubt if the introduction service had tried to match her according to the characteristics that she had requested —income, height, marital status, occupation, religious background—or if only age and height and sex were the criteria.

Unless he or she just "falls into" an ideal situation, it will be necessary for the single man or woman to date. Unfortunately, most singles that I spoke to told me that even the word *dating* conjured up negative images. Singles in their twenties, I observed, have an easier time dating if their relationships from adolescence on were healthy and open ones. If dating was a problem for them then, it will probably continue to be as they get older. Older singles expressed to me their need to change past dating patterns, but their inability to do so. When one man who was used to instant intimacy finally decided to rule out sex, initially, in forming a relationship and see if a friendship could first develop with the woman to whom he was attracted, his early anxiety was soon replaced by exhilaration. "At thirty," he explained, "I realized that none of the women I have known, or lived with, have been my friends. We've had great sex, but something else was missing. But I never knew how to go about getting it." He continued not to; I soon learned that his non-sex relationship dissolved.

I found, most often, that never-married singles described relationships in the future tense—"my ideal marriage (or relationship) would be"—whereas once-married singles (who were not widowed) detailed what they did *not* want a relationship or marriage to be.

Singles who substitute activities for intimacy are faced with heavy bills. "I have to find meaning in activities rather than in growing with somebody else," a thirty-eight-year-old woman explains. "That can get expensive." A thirty-one-year-old graduate student wishes she had someone she loved with whom to spend evenings at home. "Then I could study more, because that's what I really want to do. But I know I'm not going to meet anyone by sitting in my apartment so I have to get out there, and that usually means spending money. I don't like eating home alone, so that means restaurants, unless I'm taken out, and more expense." Some singles overextend their funds for the sake of the "hunt." Hoping to meet someone, they may spend $1,000 on a one-week vacation that they can ill afford. Two *can* live cheaper than one. Even professional men are rooming with each other because of the financial strain of spiraling rents. But at the age of thirty or forty, unless one is a homosexual, living with a same-sex roommate or two is surely not what it's all about. Perhaps the most whimsical complaint about the economic toll of being single was this comment from a twenty-six-year-old bank teller: "If I cook dinner, there are too many leftovers!" A forty-year-old man echoed her gripe: "Frozen vegetable packages are always too much for just me, and I haven't figured out how to store the extra." (Interestingly enough, big business is, even in this area, jumping on the singles bandwagon. Many types of packaged foods are now being remarketed in single portions.)

Certainly few would advocate marriage or cohabitation just because statistics indicate that married persons have fewer physical and emotional problems than singles. Being single does not automatically mean that one will experience emotional difficulties or will die younger. When someone who is single wishes to be otherwise—and the problem is not in meeting the "right one," but in being able to tolerate intimacy—that person might consider outside help. Deciding which situation actually confronts the single—a practical problem of not having found a suitable potential mate or a deeper problem of personal intolerance of closeness and its other side, separation—is a hard determination for the single, or his or her family and friends, to make. If living alone is accompanied by overeating, smoking, excessive dependence on friends and family, an inability to adapt to suitable levels of intimacy or distance—that single might be crying out for help.

One would presume that after ten, twenty, thirty, or more years of singleness, most singles would have figured out a way not to be single, or to enjoy that state. Some, of course, do; but many, whether they are thirty or seventy years old, remain in its lonely grip.

# 8

⇾⋙⇾⋙⇾⋙

# *The Best of Both Worlds*

Our culture finds it easier to promote singleness than to offer guidance to singles who wish to be otherwise. Magazines and movies demonstrate the wonders of solitude at the same fevered pitch as they once romanticized the delights of dancing cheek to cheek. The singles industry capitalizes on the loneliness of the single and his or her wish for self-esteem and acceptance. It presents a world in which success, love, friends, admirers, and happiness abound, though such a description is equally false for the world of marriage. Perhaps the mushrooming of divorce in the 1970s reflected the disillusionment of those who had accepted the media glorification of family in the late 1950s and the 60s, upon discovering that marriage had neither brightened their teeth nor ensured their happiness.

As singleness became "in" in the 1970s, the media downplayed some of the evidence of the physical and psychological consequences of isolation. The effects of singleness are far more pervasive than "not being able to finish a quart of milk before it goes sour." It is as detrimental to gloss over the drawbacks of singleness as it is to dwell on them. Although the unattached single appears to be independent, I have discovered that singles are, indeed, quite dependent—on their parents, on their siblings, on their work, on their friends, on their pets, and, when involved in a relationship, on their partner of the moment.

Many unattached singles are still inordinately tied to their parents. A man of forty calls his mother twice a week, even though she lives in another city, and has to inform her every time he goes on a bi-weekly business trip. When he visited his New England hometown, and brought his new girlfriend, he decided not to introduce her to his mother. Instead, his girlfriend sat in their hotel room while mother and son had dinner together. A dancer is awakened by her mother's daily six A.M. calls. The dancer then reports all the details of her social engagements of the previous evening; her mother provides explicit advice on what to say and do in business and personal situations. When the dancer moves in with her boyfriend, the morning calls from Mother persist, despite the boyfriend's protests. A man in his late twenties told me that he was so anxious to see his girl after three weeks of separation that he arrived over an hour early. Yet he told her that he would be unable to stay the night because he had to visit his mother early the next morning. When I asked a man in his late thirties with what woman he had had his longest relationship, he replied, half-jokingly, "My mother." For some, this bond interferes with the establishment of intimate ties outside the family. As the father of a divorced woman said at a family gathering, "I don't want Jessica to remarry. I want her all to myself."

The single person tends to lean heavily on his or her siblings. A single man in his early forties, who considers his brother his best friend, told me he had accused a divorced woman with whom he was involved of seeing her sister too often. " 'So what?' " she replied. " 'I've been lonely. Besides, I love my sister and I enjoy her company. There have been times when we've been separated for years.' " Marg, a single woman in her mid-thirties, explained that her younger sister was living with her until she found her own apartment. Marg confessed that she noticed that her social life dwindled after her sister's arrival. "I may be temporarily relieved of my loneliness, but I'm losing time trying to find a man," she says. Similarly, Carla, a single woman in her early thirties, drifts into dinners with one of her five siblings whenever she does not have a date. "Instead, I should be trying to find someone," Carla says, "but it's so difficult—and frightening. And I know I'll always be welcome, and have a good time, with my brothers or sisters."

The strong support network of close friends that saves the unattached and, especially, the living-alone single from total isolation may prove a mixed blessing. When friendships make demands on the time and emotions of a single, and he or she gets gratifications from the investment, he or she may lack the hours, energy, or impetus to pursue a long-term romantic relationship. I have met singles who filled every weekday night with a different friend. On weekends they visited out-of-town friends and thus avoided the weekend-alone syndrome.

Wendy, a divorced woman in her late twenties, found she had so many girlfriends that she did not have a free evening in the next two weeks for a dinner date with a man she had recently met. Bill, a divorced professor in his late forties, realized that he had cultivated so many companions to have dinner with that he lacked the time to find someone with whom he could become romantically involved. Bill also confessed that he feels he is paying the price for a life that has overemphasized work.

Those singles who are disheartened by their inability to find "the one" often have exaggerated needs for affection. When they do enter an intimate relationship, they make excessive demands on their partners. They become overly dependent, many times on someone who does not want it, or cannot handle it. Susan met Wayne at a bar. They left together, married two months later, and have been inseparable ever since. A single man in his thirties told me that he resented the fact that his girlfriend wanted to talk to him at least every other day. On the other hand, a married woman does not interpret her husband's phone call to inform her that he will be late as a sign of dependence as much as an indication of "common courtesy," as she described it.

Unattached singles who have an excessive need for love live in a feast-or-famine situation. Unless they come to terms with this problem, these "needy" singles are condemned to a lifetime of short-lived relationships, and will scare off most potential mates. A woman in her thirties finds it harder to separate after a date than to be alone. A waitress becomes so distraught when her boyfriend has to leave her at the end of their weekend together that he has learned to preface their togetherness with an announcement of which Sunday train he must take, thereby providing her with ample time to prepare for his departure. A widow confronts her boyfriend at the start of each weekly date with the question "So when are we going to get together again?" One man found that when he was twenty-nine he had to decide between his new job and his girlfriend because he was unable to focus on both simultaneously. Twelve years later, he still had the job, and he was still single and alone.

In these and other ways, unattached singles who are unable to find a satisfactory romantic relationship reveal certain adolescent traits. They want a relationship when they want it, and on their own terms. They are unable, or unwilling, to compromise. George refuses to make a date a week in advance because he feels "restricted." Predictably, he is frequently without a date on Saturday nights since few women will, for long, tolerate his laissez-faire life-style. George does, however, find that he can usually pick a woman up at a singles bar and, temporarily, satisfy his need for physical closeness. Margaret unceasingly talks about herself whenever someone new takes her to dinner. Her self-centeredness, which might have been typical when she was fifteen, is inappropriate at fifty. Unattached singles are still sorting out their identities. It is not uncommon for them to be asking: "Do I really want to get married and settle down?" "Do I really want to be a parent?" These questions from singles well past their twenties are more typically heard from teenagers. Unfortunately, until the unattached single finds his or her own identity, he or she will not be able confidently to decide on a mate. "Why aren't you married yet?" I asked a woman who has been living with her boyfriend for seven years. "He's being supported by his parents," she answered. "Somehow that just doesn't seem like the way to start off a marriage." Her boyfriend is close to thirty and back in school, trying out his third career choice. A woman in her early thirties who has never married shared her recent thoughts on how her singleness might be tied to her self-centeredness: "I've certainly enjoyed being single . . . so far," she began. "There is real flexibility and fun. Of course it's all self-serving and selfish. I mean, everything I do is just for myself. But that's fun too. We're all basically selfish, and I'm more selfish than most."

Singles who live alone find that their self-centeredness increases with time. "It's like looking up your ass," one single woman explained. "All you do is eat yourself up alive. It's as if you are the whole world and no one else really matters." A distorted perspective about oneself is also possible if there is no one to react to one's ideas and experiences. "I'm either too big or too small," says a man in his forties.

A black man in Philadelphia, who is in his late twenties, echoes these sentiments: "I plan to avoid marriage as long as I can. Until all the playing is out of my system. I don't want to make somebody unhappy by having them wait for me at home. I'm not ready for marriage. When I'm tired and I want to settle down with a woman, that's when I'll do it. I find life alone lonely at times, and rewarding at others. It's lonely when you want someone there and all the ladies that you call are occupied. It's rewarding to live alone when you don't have to go through the nagging-wife routine or worry about anyone but yourself; when you don't have to worry about buying kids shoes and you don't have to answer to anyone but yourself. There's no one there but you." A Manhattan woman who earns $18,000 a year and is twenty-eight expresses similar anti-marriage views. "I love the freedom of being single. Coming home to my own apartment and doing whatever I want, when I want. I don't mind living with someone on the weekends, period. But the thought of being married and coming home every night to the same person and cooking and cleaning for two people. I can't even cook and clean for myself!"

Betty, a married woman in her mid-thirties who lives in Madison, Wisconsin, with her husband and daughter, compares being single to adolescence. She spent her college years in Washington, D.C., and was single in the 1960s. "I did the whole career-girl bit, with the apartment in Georgetown, et cetera. I married at twenty-seven. I didn't enjoy being single. It was remarkably like the novel *Sheila Levine Is Dead and Living in New York.* I was desperate to get married. I hated 'dating'—I am a one-relationship type. In a way, being single is like being back in high school. The dating, the emphasis on 'personal growth,' the rites of passage of marriage and divorce—when I read about it (and it's difficult to read about much else now, with the flood of confessional literature) I'm struck by how much it sounds like my junior high and high school diaries. The agonies! The emotions! The self-analysis! The point is: how much of that can a human being take? Maybe people get married to have a rest from all the *Stürm und Drang?* Maybe that is marriage's function in today's world?"

Singles have a misguided concentration on singleness

rather than on the dynamics of a relationship. Staying single should not become a primary concern for any man or woman, for even if he masters singleness—even if she conquers aloneness and loneliness—the single has won the wrong battle. The battle is not in conquering singleness, but in redefining and conquering togetherness. A woman of thirty who has been single since her divorce seven years ago, finds it difficult to stay "involved" with the man whom she loves. Part of her wants to flee—and retreat to the familiar womb of aloneness. "Sometimes, when he says he wants to get to know me better," she told me, "I automatically assume that means he wants to get to see the 'real me' so he can reject me. It is so much easier—at least in the short run—to bemoan my singleness and how 'no one understands me and loves me for myself'—than it is to allow this caring, giving man to get closer and closer to me. I guess I'm learning that it isn't the way I thought it would be—that he likes you, you like him, and, boom, everything is instantly solved."

Despite all evidence to the contrary, some singles stubbornly cling to the idea that *only* luck determines whether or not someone remains single. "If I'm lucky," an unmarried woman of thirty-four told me, "I could find the 'right one' in San Francisco, where there are more gays than straights. But I'm unlucky. So even in this city—overflowing with eligible men—I can't find anyone. But I don't blame myself, any more than a sailor in the middle of the ocean could blame himself for lacking a woman." Luck *is* involved, but there are individual and social conditions that are just as important in explaining why one is single. A thirty-year-old divorced woman called her mother with the good news: "I've met a really sweet eligible man and he likes me." Her mother answered, "You see that. I always said it was being at the right place at the right time." But her daughter disagreed. "That's just part of it. Because ten years ago I would not have even given him the time of day. Now I want to give him the time of his life. Before, I was looking for the glitter. I was so overanxious about having a relationship, I wouldn't have let him take *my* phone number. I would have taken his. Two years of therapy have changed my view of myself, and of relationships, and that has a lot more to do with it than luck."

The sense of hopelessness displayed by some singles can be very destructive. "There's no one out there for me," was a common refrain that singles over the age of thirty-five shared with me. How much of that was self-fulfilling prophecy? As in most areas of life, success breeds success. One positive date often leads to a second. Going to parties, and enjoying oneself, often opens up new potential dates—and more parties and more dates. Some singles become so "soured" on relationships that they discount even the possibility of romance. "You know why I'm looking forward to meeting that lawyer on Tuesday night?" a single woman in her late twenties asked me. "Because if he is even somewhat tolerable, it might mean that I'll have a date for New Year's Eve. Then my mother won't bug me." Since it was only the beginning of November, I felt saddened that the possibility of a relationship was not at issue; having a date for New Year's Eve—to some still a symbol of an active social life—was of greater importance.

The majority of singles that I interviewed, however, *do* want relationships. Be it love, an intimate union, an equal partnership based on mutuality and trust, a living-together arrangement, a steady sexual partner, or marriage, everyone is able to state what, ideally, he or she wants in his or her personal life. I have found that almost all singles, no matter how content they are living alone, fantasize about someday having a special partner. Even if the union desired was one of living together, rather than marriage, it is always, for heterosexuals, a one-on-one vision. It did not matter how long a man or woman had been single, or how bitter he or she was from a divorce. As one single man in his mid-forties said to me, "I always want to keep that door open, even though I'm perfectly happy the way I am now." Of course friends or work may compensate if a lover is unavailable, but that simply does not replace an intimate romantic relationship—"someone to share the joys, or sorrow," as one never-married man in his mid-fifties who doesn't mind being alone put it. And as one divorced woman explained to me: "I remember that when something unexpected happened after I broke up with the person I'd been living with, I wanted to share the news. I found that I had to call five friends in order to get the same amount of feedback that I previously would have received from him alone."

"I was single, without a husband or children to answer to," a divorced woman in her early thirties told me. "I was free, to play, travel, and work to the extent my income and inclinations allowed. But it was far from the glamorous and unending pleasure-seeking that my attached friends suspected. When my social life became too time consuming or predictable, I retreated to my work, my hobbies, and my fantasies, to business trips alone, or nights out with my girlfriends." An eighteen-year-old college freshman says, "It would be a neat idea to have someone I could have sex with, whenever I wanted to. Someone to share my problems and happiness with." "My brother just got married for the first time," a cab driver told me. "He's forty-four. He had this exciting bachelor existence in California. He was often written up in the gossip columns about dating this or that actress. But when he'd visit me, he'd say, 'You know, Murray, this is what life is all about. A wife, kids, a few close friends.'"

If singles want to be coupled but are unable to be so, is it because they lack opportunity? Or is it that they have unrealistic notions about marriage (as all-consuming) and singleness (as the quintessence of independence)? The majority of disgruntled singles that I interviewed believe that they lack the opportunity to meet eligible mates; those who were happy being single felt that the opportunities were there, but not taken advantage of. The reality is somewhere in between. It is harder to meet eligible partners when one is forty than when one is twenty, but if one's attitude is unrealistic, it would be irrelevant if five suitors were to appear on one's doorstep.

Unattached singles may fantasize about the ideal partner, but rarely do they consider how their ideal might differ from reality, or why their choices so often fall so short of their ideals. As one woman in her early thirties, who is trying again with her boyfriend after a year's separation, said to me: "We've both grown up in the last year. I'm not picking on him as much anymore. I'm not looking for perfection. I'm not as unrealistic. I accept him. Sure he has a bad temper, but it's over in five minutes. I'm looking at what's right about Sam, rather than what's wrong."

Unwilling singles are frequently unaware of the misconceptions about relationships that hamper them from finding "the right one." Quite often, they report an extended history of being in love with someone who did not return the feeling or being loved by someone whom they did not want. "It was mostly pretty one-sided for a while," a forty-year-old never-married man who lives alone told me. In recalling his previous relationships, he reminded me of the adolescent who lusts for his chemistry teacher. "I saw her for quite a while. Maybe you can call it an obsession. I was literally insane about her. Insane. I couldn't get enough of her. When she would come to my apartment—and I knew she was coming to my apartment that night at the appointed hour—I would start pacing an hour before she arrived. Thinking what she was going to smell like. What she was going to taste like. What she was going to feel like. Everything about her. It was bad." Other unwilling singles have tales of "what he (or she) did to me" as they relive short- and longer-term affairs that did not lead to marriage. An objective listener wonders, "Why didn't he (she) get out of the relationship after a month?" Or "Didn't you see that he (she) was a bad marital risk?" But these unwilling singles are unable to see the destructive patterns to their love lives, or, if they do, are unable to alter the cycles.

Not only do singles have unrealistic notions about marriage and coupling, they also labor under misconceptions about parenting. One widower, who placed an ad in a newspaper to solicit dates, told me he was astounded at the glowing way that the single women who answered his ad (which had noted that he had a daughter) described parenting. "It was as if they were running down a field of flowers with a big banner labeled 'parenting.' Those women talked about the 'joys of motherhood' in such a way that it was obvious they had never been a parent. I wondered if they ever would be willing to put up with the work that parenting really entails."

Another reason that singles fail to find the right partners is that they are reluctant to take the time, and make the effort, to continue the search. The problem today, and one of the reasons for the increase in singleness, is not the need to fulfill the dream of having it all—independence, intimacy, career, family—but the need to select a partner whose idea of a good relationship is complementary to one's own. Because there are now so many choices—singleness, living together, marriage, parenting—it is impossible to assume that all men want children or that all women want to work (or even that all women want children and all men want to marry). The fact is that only 7 percent of the 57 million families in the United States today conform to the *Father Knows Best* formula—working father, stay-at-home mother with two children.

Much has changed since the 1940s, when my parents got married. My father was away in the army, so my mother was able to attend college, graduate, and start teaching. But after he returned, she got pregnant, and soon gave up her job. Was there any plausible alternative? Back then, it was rare for middle-class married ladies to work. For the next thirteen years she was a housewife, chauffeur, and mother of three. Occasionally she assisted my father at his dental office, but most of the time she was "overworked and under pressure because she did not enjoy the business of running a household," as my father recently explained it to me. I vividly remember what a jolt it was when she resumed teaching. My mother had exams to prepare for and courses to take. My sister and I had to share the responsibility of cleaning the house and preparing dinner. Suddenly my father was the one who came to our class plays. But the improvement in my mother's temperament made us all wish she had gone back to work sooner.

Today over 50 percent of married women are working. A woman need not remain single in order to pursue her career. Although complete role reversals are still rare—stay-at-home parenting fathers and full-time, non-parenting working wives—it is more possible than ever before to find the kind of man or woman who will allow each partner to pursue his or her interests. Times *have* changed. A woman of thirty-four, who has never married, remarked to me how few options there seemed to be when she graduated from college: "You got married when you got out of college. The husbands were the principal breadwinners. The women had babies. Or you could get a teaching job or a second-rate job or become a nurse—until you got married. The term *liberated woman* didn't even come up till four years after I graduated from college. I know only one woman who chose to get her Ph.D. rather than marry some guy. She got her Ph.D., married Carl, the doctor, had a baby, and her career is slowly moving along. If I had only been born seven years later, I would have found men who shared my progressive attitude toward marriage."

How does one go about choosing the right partner?

"I'm amazed at the important decisions I made when I was only twenty-three," a bank executive who has been married for almost five years told me. "Somehow I picked John out, and I've never regretted it. And I was a pretty miserable sixteen-year-old without too much of a social life." Others, far older, are still struggling to find someone who conforms to their notions of romance and friendship. Still others have given up and believe they will never find the right partner. Early childhood factors are important in the mate-selection process. If a man or woman was raised in a household that failed to offer a good model for intimacy, it will be difficult for him or her to create it for himself. Divorced singles often told me that it was only after years of analysis that they realized they had unwittingly sought out, achieved, and later rejected a relationship that was a replica of the negative interaction of their parents' marriage. With relationships, as with history, if you do not understand the past, you are condemned to relive it. A woman in her mid-twenties who has remarried and does not want children says: "I loved my parents very much but left home, and never came back, when I was sixteen because we didn't get along. My mother was too dominating, self-righteous, and I was stifled. I soon realized that my first husband, to whom I was married for ten months, was very much like my mother. But my second husband is a lot kinder toward me."

A majority of singles have trouble not only in choosing the right partner but in playing the dating game. "What should I do if I feel attracted to a man who is not available?" a single woman in her mid-thirties asked me. "Why do you think Sid didn't call me back?" another single woman inquired. "I can't understand why she's suddenly busy on Saturday nights," a single man in his late twenties complained. These and similar questions illustrate how naïve singles often are about the "rules" of dating. "Where do you find out what's right when it comes to relationships?" a single woman asked. "Is it in Emily Post? Amy Vanderbilt? Werner Erhard?" Most men and women learn the "rules" by the age of fifteen. They observe the interactions that are appropriate in social situations and experiment with techniques and behavior patterns that either work or fail. Those that work, they continue to use; those that fail, they discard. Unattached singles without a special relationship in their lives often are still employing behavior patterns that repeatedly fail. They stubbornly cling to false notions about male/female relationships, often claiming, "I refuse to 'play the game.' "

A married couple that I know who live in Evanston, Illinois, refer to themselves as "dinosaurs," because they have been happily together for twenty years. Have we become so cynical about marriage that those who fail to become divorce statistics are almost as extinct as dinosaurs? Has the pendulum swung so far in the other direction that a worthy ideal such as "for better or worse" has been replaced with "till divorce do you part"? This widespread cynicism about marriage is grist for the mill of the disgruntled single. Some singles avoid the pleasure of marriage because they fear divorce or the death of a spouse. As a divorced woman in her thirties explained: "Marriage is forever to me. I failed once. It took four years to work through all the changes that becoming single again necessitated. From time to time, I have a man. But I have a stability in my life that I will not relinquish for the myth of to-getherness. Yet there's a side of me that wants to be a parent, and I still dream of sharing that experience." A banker in his late thirties offers a similar perspective: "I take the vows of marriage very seriously. Perhaps too seriously. And I think that is one of the reasons I have never yet felt sure enough to marry anyone."

Another single woman, in justifying her aloneness, recounted the life of her friend's uncle: "He married at twenty and it was a disaster. Eight years later he divorced, and his wife went to Mexico with his two children. When the children reached their late teens, she sent them back to him and he raised them until they left home. Then he met his second wife, and about five years ago, she died of cancer. Then, about three years later, he met his third wife. And he just learned that she has something wrong with her, and it's probably also terminal cancer. At least I've been spared that kind of life by living alone these past fifteen years."

The major fear of unattached singles is of relationships. They need help in learning how to establish, develop, and maintain a fulfilling interdependence with someone else. As one New York psychiatrist noted: "If by one's thirties there has been a pattern of short-term relationships with the 'wrong ones,' factors other than just bad luck may be involved."

Most of the committed singles that I interviewed believe that a permanent relationship requires a partial renunciation of treasured personal goals. The complaint that I consistently heard (which I believe accounts for a great deal of the unattached singleness today) is that marriage involves relinquishing individual freedom, independence, and self-reliance. Singles fear the loss of self in a relationship, and the unison of marriage is scorned. Marriage is equated with "pressure" and "loss of freedom." This attitude appeared often to be based on one unhappy personal experience, on a misapprehension, dating from childhood, of the marital relationship, or on observations of other couples—colored by the single's own limited experience. As one single man in his seventies told me, "My friend says 'to me marriage stinks, but it's better than being single.' I feel that the disadvantage of marriage is that it is often an endless effort to please a partner who cannot be pleased." Other singles are more insightful about their limited understanding of what goes into a successful intimate relationship. "I've never known a good relationship," a divorced woman explains, "so I don't even know what I should be looking for." "The longest I've maintained an interest in a woman," one single man confided, "is nine months."

The American culture is unique in its overemphasis of the marital couple as a unit, a united front against the world. Counselor Marcia Lasswell and her co-author Norman Lobsenz observe that in most other cultures, marital partners are freer to have separate identities, individual friendships, and personal interests. The struggle for separateness, they note, is often seen in this country as an indication that a marriage is on the rocks, rather than as a sign of personal growth.

For the incidence of singleness to decrease, false illusions about marriage must be dispelled just as must distorted notions about the single's life. In her analysis of the advice handed out twenty-five years ago in popular magazines, Virginia Kidd notes that togetherness was the message of the 1950s. "The happy marriage bubbled along in a sea of 'togetherness,' " she writes, "of 'shared hobbies, shared books, shared evenings in the basement refinishing old furniture or intending to work on the rumpus room and playing table tennis instead! Shared serving—in the Boy or Girl Scouts, Sunday school, the PTA.' *Better Homes and Gardens* depicted family solidarity so great 'you don't even want a night out.' Those who did want a night out had 'troubled' marriages." Furthermore, Kidd writes, "Given their basic sexual personalities, sane individuals married. People who didn't want to get married had 'marriage phobias' and needed psychiatric help. *Newsweek* described their plight in a 1956 article, reporting 20 cases that fortunately had happy endings: 'With psychotherapy, all 20 lost their complexes and married.' "

For a while, it seemed the only solution for those who were disenchanted with their mates was to discount marriage completely. The institutions of marriage and the family were suddenly deromanticized—*The Female Eunuch, The Second Sex,* and the women's movement helped the process along—and a new myth was created, of exalted singleness. The 1960s was the "Do your own thing" era and the 1970s was the period of "How do you cope with all this freedom?" Must marriage be the choking togetherness of the 1950s? Is the only alternative singleness? The solution, as usual, is far from simple. Everyone—married or single—is able to find benefits and drawbacks to each; neither is perhaps ideal.

The majority of unattached singles that I interviewed espoused a fear of choking intimacy. To them, commitment meant being in a relationship that demanded loss of freedom. Those who feared intimacy consistently picked "the wrong" partners. In this vicious cycle, they never had to test their myths about an intimate relationship. They concerned themselves with finding the "perfect" partner *next time,* rather than striving for autonomy and interdependence within the relationship *this time.* Occasionally a single would realize that his or her fear of intimacy was at the bottom of his or her poor selection of potential mates: "I've never found the right one because I wasn't psychologically ready for marriage," as a thirty-year-old single woman put it. Generally, the connection between fear of intimacy and thwarted love relationships was not made. "I don't need a man," or "I like being alone," was the most frequent retort to the question of why someone was not in love.

Unattached singles who fear intimacy may still ostensibly be involved in the search for a mate, but their fear of intimacy prevents them from finding the right one or reading situations accurately. For example, a single woman spends all her time at a party—where there are several eligible men—talking to a married man. Later, she is disturbed to find out that he is unavailable; yet his wedding band was clearly displayed. By contrast, another single woman, wishing to find the right one, "interviewed" all the single males at a party until she met one who was a possibility. Those who were neurotic, married, or negative were sized up and bypassed. Singles who fear intimacy may also behave in such inappropriate ways when they do find "the right one," that the intimacy is short-lived. For example, they have sex before it is appropriate. A woman will perform services, such as cleaning a man's apartment or cooking dinner, before any commitment is given. A man will treat the woman he supposedly cares for in such an oppressive manner that she is compelled to leave him. A woman who finally finds a man she likes will have a party and invite several of her ex-lovers as well as her new beau. A man who fears intimacy will unwittingly display his bad side to his new date, but later regrets his inability to undo that unfavorable impression. More examples of the single's fear of intimacy abound:

> A thirty-two-year-old college instructor does not date any woman for longer than a month "whether I like her or not."

> Joel, who is in his early thirties, is firmly against marriage. He tells the women that he likes, before they get involved, that that is his philosophy. Joel's relationships usually last from one to three years; the breakup is facilitated by the woman's wish to marry and his reiteration of his unshakable anti-marriage views.

> After his wife left him, Victor, a man in his mid-forties, consistently dated women in their early twenties. His pattern of little more than one-night stands has persisted for the last five years.

> Meg is so afraid of intimacy that she finds herself uncomfortable in the role of "woman." She dresses, and behaves, either like a child or like a matron. As a result, the young man who is sincerely interested in her finds himself being "turned off" by her behavior. Yet Meg

wants to change, and grow closer to her friend, because the "woman" side—that is buried within—craves intimacy.

Carl, who is soon to be divorced, is so blatantly aggressive in his approach—"Your place or mine?"—that neither an evening of sex nor a relationship follows.

Carol begins talking about marriage on her third date, scaring men away by such inappropriate pressure on a new relationship.

The increased acceptability of remaining, or becoming, an unattached single camouflages the need of these single adults to understand their fears of intimacy. It is the singles who pay a high price. They will age without the benefit of fulfilled personal romantic relationships. "Personal growth comes from interaction with people," a single man in his early thirties told me. "Someone special could be the mirror to your soul." Nevertheless, some unattached single men and women feel overwhelming anxiety, confusion, and distress at even the thought of sharing their lives. The combination of the increase in singleness as a permanent alternative to marriage, and the cynicism about matrimony, has discouraged these single men and women, perhaps without their realizing it, from the self-analysis needed to change the living arrangements of the rest of their lives. Indeed, they often give up the quest and settle in to their isolation and aloneness. As long as a person is not psychotic, sociopathic, or completely boring, there is something that can be learned—about oneself at the very least—by taking the chance with even a short date

*184*

with someone new. Too many singles are so fearful of commitment or so impatient to find a mature, love relationship that they avoid, or jump over, the slow, unfrenzied methods of getting to know someone. It is not uncommon today for men and women who are alone for months or years at a time to become involved in a relationship (of one to three years' duration) only to go back to complete solitude after it terminates. They gradually lose the social skills necessary for dating. They live with someone before knowing if they even want to be friends. Indeed, now that transitional singleness can last two, five, ten, or all of one's adult years, a readiness for marriage may need as much self-help and outside assistance as learning to be an independent, single person requires.

But there is a "compromise." There is a kind of singleness—a state of mind rather than a state outside matrimony—that is essential to every relationship. The old-fashioned concept of two people united against the world is no longer workable. Men and women today must play an increasing number of roles in their lifetime, and given the pressures of modern-day living, periods of solitude are almost a necessity for everyone, not just singles. "When you're married and you have children," notes a forty-two-year-old married social worker, "it's important to have time alone. I don't mean individual vacations (I don't have that), but I do mean hours, days, weekends, or friends that are not shared. Combination does not mean homogenization." Contemporary thinkers, such as sociologist Murray S. Davis, see intimacy as "distant closeness." Davis writes: "Although it is necessary for both intimates to establish a common being in order to have a personal relation of the highest order, it is not necessary for each of them to lose all individuality and become exactly like the other in the process. In fact, in acquiring a more focused ground against which to contrast himself, each intimate actually sharpens his self . . . In urbanized societies, then, personal relations permit a person to have his individuality and lose it, too."

Psychotherapist Carl Rogers advocates singleness within all relationships. He views a relationship as "a continuing process, not a contract. The work which is done is for *personal* as well as mutual satisfaction." Rogers lists, and comments on, four key elements that, from his extensive client contact, he realized are necessary for a sustained and healthy relationship: first is dedication and commitment; second, communication; third, the dissolution of roles; and fourth, becoming a separate self. "A *living* partnership is composed of two people, each of whom owns, respects, and develops his or her own selfhood," Rogers writes. He refers back to a couple, whose relationship was described earlier in his book through transcribed interviews, as one that typifies the attainment of self within intimacy. "As she becomes more and more a strong and independent self, each step in that progress aids their partnership."

Journalist Sally Wendkos Olds asks these questions about relationships: "What is the ideal marriage? Is it one in which closeness is all, composed of two best friends who share all values, do everything together and tell each other everything? Or is it one in which individuality is all, formed of two separate persons who walk parallel lines, each leading his or her own life and respecting the freedom of the other?" Olds concludes that "healthy emotional interdependence" is the answer to the extremes of separateness and choking intimacy. In that type of ideal relationship, "each person loves and values and nurtures the other and yet lets the other thrive in his or her own way."

Self-reliance and intimacy need not be mutually exclusive. It seems to me that the inability to withstand separation in, or from, a relationship can be as detrimental as the inability to tolerate intimacy. How have some singles managed to achieve autonomy—a life independent of one's romantic relationship(s)—and self-sufficiency—the ability to stand on one's own? Margaret and Jerry have been dating for over a month. They see each other one night during the week and on Saturday night. Neither their work nor their friendships are being sacrificed because of their evolving intimacy. Although they take each day at a time, they both are willing, and able, if it works out, to follow through toward a deeper commitment. Barbara is forty and a writer. Her fiancé is an inventor and businessman. She commutes to New York two days a week; the rest of the time she lives with her fiancé in a rural part of Pennsylvania. This is Barbara's second marriage and she is very positive about her relationship. But she is also realistic and knows that being in love doesn't take care of all aspects of her life. "It doesn't solve my career problems," she told me.

Combining a strong sense of self with a successful "close" relationship is no easy task. Some singles falsely believe that married or living-together couples have conquered both their loneliness and their need for freedom, independence, or self-reliance. But these couples, too, constantly redefine their own needs and, in a healthy, growing relationship, reshape their commitment to fit changing expectations. The need for "space" is a function of each man and woman, not of one particular type of relationship. "I suppose I'm living as I would like to," a thirty-two-year-old lesbian said to me, in describing her seven-year living-together arrangement, "but I would like to become a little more independent. This year my lover and I took separate vacations and it was great for both of us. But being more independent has more to do with emotional than with physical space. I would also like to be able to make more of my own friends, and I've been actively trying to do that."

Self-reliance is valuable for every adult but often unattached singles lack it. A wealthy woman of thirty-three, who recently divorced, is unable to attend an out-of-town conference because her new boyfriend will not allow her to be away in the evenings. "He sends her chocolates and flowers," her friend confided. "But it's amazing how suddenly she is unable to live her own life or do anything for herself. Why does she put up with it?" A divorced man in his early thirties is so afraid of being on his own that he maintains contact with his ex-wife, even though she is living with someone else and is soon to be married. A woman in her late thirties, who has never married and has a life that gives the appearance of independence, needs to get the opinions of three or four girlfriends before she accepts a date, goes away for a weekend, or makes almost any decision. Another single woman, a few years younger, tailors her eating habits to whether or not she has a date to pay for her meals. "Lately I've been wondering why my diet is so tied to my social life. I haven't cooked 'for myself' in years," she told me.

"I don't feel any longer that life hasn't started just because I don't have a man," one single woman explained. "Just last week I took out the sterling silver place settings that my grandmother, over the years, had given me for my trousseau. I've spent the first half of my life alone and if that's the way I spend the second half, at least I'll be using nice silverware." This single woman is redefining how she sees herself—not as half of an imaginary couple, but as a complete person deserving of respect. She is also aware that there is a next step. "I don't say that marrying or living with someone is healthier or better than living alone or just dating on a superficial level," she explains. "But there is a part of me that wants to share what still lies dormant. The major change in my perspective, however, is that I *want* to share. I don't *need* to. I'm also not *afraid* to. I've solved many of my problems, so I'm not looking for someone to rescue me. I just want to find a friend— someone who loves me as much as I love him."

# APPENDICES AND BIBLIOGRAPHY

| | 18+ # | 18+ % | 18–19 | 20–24 | 25–29 | 30–34 | 35–44 | 45–64 | 65+ |
|---|---|---|---|---|---|---|---|---|---|
| Men, 18+ | 72,716 | 100.0 | 4,017 | 9,713 | 8,812 | 7,907 | 11,940 | 20,780 | 9,548 |
| Never married | 16,970 | 23.3 | 94.9 | 67.4 | 30.2 | 14.9 | 8.3 | 6.1 | 5.4 |
| Married, spouse present | 48,233 | 66.3 | 4.2 | 28.8 | 61.4 | 73.6 | 81.0 | 83.0 | 74.6 |
| Married, spouse absent: | | | | | | | | | |
| Separated | 1,513 | 2.1 | 0.2 | 1.2 | 2.0 | 3.1 | 2.7 | 2.3 | 1.8 |
| Other | 583 | 0.8 | 0.6 | 0.9 | 0.7 | 1.0 | 0.8 | 0.8 | 0.8 |
| Widowed | 1,945 | 2.7 | — | — | 0.2 | 0.2 | 0.3 | 2.5 | 14.1 |
| Divorced | 3,471 | 4.8 | 0.1 | 1.7 | 5.5 | 7.3 | 7.0 | 5.3 | 3.3 |
| Women, 18+ | 80,629 | 100.0 | 4,184 | 10,136 | 9,128 | 8,206 | 12,671 | 22,677 | 13,627 |
| Never married | 13,644 | 16.9 | 83.1 | 49.4 | 19.6 | 9.5 | 5.9 | 4.5 | 6.1 |
| Married, spouse present | 48,129 | 59.7 | 14.2 | 43.1 | 67.0 | 74.4 | 76.5 | 71.6 | 36.9 |
| Married, spouse absent: | | | | | | | | | |
| Separated | 2,409 | 3.0 | 1.2 | 3.1 | 4.3 | 4.3 | 4.3 | 2.7 | 1.0 |
| Other | 642 | 0.8 | 0.6 | 1.1 | 0.7 | 0.8 | 0.8 | 0.8 | 0.6 |
| Widowed | 10,449 | 13.0 | — | 0.1 | 0.5 | 0.8 | 2.2 | 13.0 | 52.2 |
| Divorced | 5,355 | 6.6 | 0.9 | 3.2 | 7.8 | 10.2 | 10.4 | 7.4 | 3.3 |

SOURCE: U.S. Bureau of the Census, *Current Population Reports*, Series P-20, No. 349, "Marital Status and Living Arrangements: March 1979," Table 1.

### NEVER-MARRIED AMERICANS, BY AGE AND SEX: 1977, 1970, 1960

| Age | MALE | | | FEMALE | | |
|-----|------|------|------|------|------|------|
| | 1977 | 1970 | 1960 | 1977 | 1970 | 1960 |
| 14 to 17 years | 99.4 | 99.4 | 99.0 | 97.5 | 97.3 | 94.6 |
| 18 years | 97.5 | 95.1 | 94.6 | 84.8 | 82.0 | 75.6 |
| 19 years | 90.2 | 89.9 | 87.1 | 73.8 | 68.8 | 59.7 |
| 20 to 24 years | 63.7 | 54.7 | 53.1 | 45.3 | 35.8 | 28.4 |
| 25 to 29 years | 26.1 | 19.1 | 20.8 | 16.1 | 10.5 | 10.5 |
| 30 to 34 years | 12.2 | 9.4 | 11.9 | 7.0 | 6.2 | 6.9 |
| 35 to 39 years | 7.3 | 7.2 | 8.8 | 5.4 | 5.4 | 6.1 |
| 40 to 44 years | 6.9 | 6.3 | 7.3 | 4.7 | 4.9 | 6.1 |
| 45 to 54 years | 5.6 | 7.5 | 7.4 | 4.2 | 4.9 | 7.0 |
| 55 to 64 years | 5.8 | 7.8 | 8.0 | 4.6 | 6.8 | 8.0 |
| 65 years and over | 5.9 | 7.5 | 7.7 | 6.4 | 7.7 | 8.5 |

SOURCE: U.S. Bureau of the Census, *Marital Status and Living Arrangements: March 1977*, p. 1.

### SUICIDE RATES BY SEX AND MARITAL STATUS, 15–19 YEARS, UNITED STATES, 1959–61, PER 100,000 POPULATION

| | | Never-married | Married |
|-----|-----|------|------|
| 15 TO 19 YEARS | Male | 5.2 | 7.9 |
| | Female | 1.4 | 2.4 |

SOURCE: Dr. Richard H. Seiden, University of California, Berkeley, personal communication.

## Estimated Proportions of Couples Who Celebrate Selected Wedding Anniversaries

| Wedding Anniversary | PROPORTION WHO CELEBRATE THE ANNIVERSARY AFTER— | |
| --- | --- | --- |
| | First Marriage | Remarriage |
| 5th | 5 of every 6 | 4 of every 5 |
| 10th | 4 of every 5 | 3 of every 4 |
| 20th | 3 of every 4 | 1 of every 2 |
| 30th | 2 of every 3 | 1 of every 3 |
| 35th | 1 of every 2 | 1 of every 5 |
| 40th | 2 of every 5 | 1 of every 8 |
| 45th | 1 of every 3 | 1 of every 15 |
| 50th | 1 of every 5 | 1 of every 20 |
| 55th | 1 of every 10 | 1 of every 50 |
| 60th | 1 of every 20 | 1 of every 100 |
| 65th | 1 of every 50 | very rare |
| 70th | 1 of every 100 | very rare |

SOURCE: Paul C. Glick and Arthur J. Norton, "Marrying, Divorcing, and Living Together in the U.S. Today," *Population Bulletin*, 32 (Washington, D.C.: Population Reference Bureau, 1977, updated reprint, 1979), p. 14.

RATIO OF DEATH RATES OF SINGLE, WIDOWED, AND
DIVORCED TO MARRIED PERSONS,* FOR CORONARY HEART
DISEASE, UNITED STATES, 1959–1961

| | MALE | | | FEMALE | | |
|---|---|---|---|---|---|---|
| Age | Single | Wid-owed | Di-vorced | Single | Wid-owed | Di-vorced |
| White | | | | | | |
| 15 and over, | | | | | | |
| age adjusted | 1.34 | 1.51 | 1.79 | 1.22 | 1.45 | 1.32 |
| 25–34 | 1.52 | 1.98 | 2.83 | 3.17 | 5.17 | 2.28 |
| 35–44 | 1.47 | 1.84 | 2.47 | 2.08 | 2.34 | 2.14 |
| 45–54 | 1.39 | 1.66 | 2.16 | 1.33 | 1.69 | 1.60 |
| 55–64 | 1.28 | 1.55 | 1.92 | 1.03 | 1.48 | 1.30 |
| 65–74 | 1.37 | 1.45 | 1.67 | 1.05 | 1.35 | 1.20 |
| 75–84 | 1.35 | 1.39 | 1.56 | 1.26 | 1.35 | 1.32 |
| 85 and above | 1.27 | 1.35 | 1.37 | 1.63 | 1.56 | 1.40 |
| Nonwhite | | | | | | |
| 15 and over, | | | | | | |
| age adjusted | 1.53 | 2.07 | 1.88 | 1.39 | 1.94 | 1.37 |
| 25–34 | 2.24 | 4.24 | 2.64 | 1.61 | 2.37 | 1.26 |
| 35–44 | 2.04 | 2.61 | 2.42 | 1.83 | 2.42 | 1.35 |
| 45–54 | 1.77 | 2.65 | 2.32 | 1.39 | 2.15 | 1.40 |
| 55–64 | 1.33 | 2.24 | 1.91 | 1.15 | 2.08 | 1.39 |
| 65–74 | 1.46 | 1.83 | 1.79 | 1.40 | 1.87 | 1.39 |
| 75–84 | 1.55 | 1.59 | 1.49 | 1.39 | 1.56 | 1.33 |
| 85 and above | 1.42 | 1.58 | 1.73 | 1.91 | 1.91 | 1.29 |

* The ratios for married individuals would be 1.00 in all cases.

SOURCE: James J. Lynch, *The Broken Heart* (New York: Basic
Books, 1977, 1979), p. 51.

AGE-ADJUSTED SUICIDE RATES BY MARITAL STATUS,
UNITED STATES POPULATION, 15 YEARS AND OLDER, 1959–61,
PER 100,000 POPULATION

| Married | Divorced | Widowed | Never-married |
|---------|----------|---------|---------------|
| 11.9 | 39.9 | 48.0 | 20.9 |

SOURCE: Dr. Richard H. Seiden, University of California, Berkeley, personal communication.


WOMEN WHOSE FIRST MARRIAGE ENDED IN WIDOWHOOD
BY AGE AT WIDOWHOOD, PERCENT REMARRIED, AND
MEDIAN YEARS WIDOWED AT SURVEY DATE: JUNE 1975

| Age at Widowhood | Number (in thousands) | Percent Remarried | Median Years Widowed |
|------------------|------------------------|-------------------|----------------------|
| 14 to 29 | 1,143 | 77* | 7* |
| 30 to 39 | 1,090 | 49 | 4 |
| 40 to 49 | 1,436 | 27 | 11 |
| 50 to 75 | 3,107 | 6 | 9 |
| Total | 6,778 | 30 | — |

* Rounded off to the nearest whole number.

SOURCE: S. R. Hiltz, "Widowhood: A Roleless Role," *Marriage & Family Review* 1 (Nov./Dec. 1978), p. 3.

## PROPORTION OF AMERICAN WOMEN WHO ARE WIDOWS, BY AGE, 1976

| Age Group | Percentage Widows |
|-----------|-------------------|
| Under 35 | 1 |
| 35–39 | 2* |
| 40–44 | 3 |
| 45–54 | 7 |
| 55–64 | 19 |
| 65–74 | 42 |
| 75+ | 70 |

*\* Rounded off to the nearest whole number.*

SOURCE: S. R. Hiltz, "Widowhood: A Roleless Role," *Marriage & Family Review* 1 (Nov./Dec. 1978), p. 3.

## AGE OF PARTNERS IN TWO-PERSON UNMARRIED-COUPLE HOUSEHOLDS, 1978
### (*Numbers in thousands*)

| Age of Man | TOTAL | Age of Woman 14 TO 24 YEARS | 25 TO 44 YEARS | 45 TO 64 YEARS | 65 YEARS AND OVER |
|---|---|---|---|---|---|
| Total | 865 | 218 | 423 | 155 | 70 |
| 14 to 24 years | 359 | 192 | 164 | 3 | — |
| 25 to 44 years | 280 | 17 | 228 | 33 | 2 |
| 45 to 64 years | 128 | 5 | 25 | 78 | 21 |
| 65 years and over | 97 | 4 | 4 | 41 | 48 |
| Percent* | 100.0 | 25.2 | 48.9 | 17.9 | 8.1 |
| 14 to 24 years | 41.5 | 22.2 | 19.0 | 0.3 | — |
| 25 to 44 years | 32.4 | 2.0 | 26.4 | 3.8 | 0.2 |
| 45 to 64 years | 14.8 | 0.6 | 2.9 | 9.0 | 2.4 |
| 65 years and over | 11.2 | 0.5 | 0.5 | 4.7 | 5.5 |

* *All percentages are derived from the base of 865,000 two-person unmarried-couple households.*

SOURCE: U.S. Bureau of the Census, *Marital Status and Living Arrangements: March 1978*, p. 4.

# Bibliography

This book is based primarily on hundreds of anonymous interviews and questionnaires. I am grateful to all those—named and concealed—whose valuable time and insights enabled me to write this book. I am particularly appreciative to those directors of programs for singles who not only granted me extensive interviews but also agreed to contact their clients for participation in my study. A special thanks to Marcia Goldenberg, Jean Barish, Nona Aguilar, Marsha Porcell, Ginny Mugavero, Alex Hatcher, Robert Flint, Steven Conn, Lynn Mullins, Judy Cestaro, Maxine Wallach, Eileen and Richard Hoffman, and especially Barbara Anderman and Dr. Steven Gruenberg.

Included in the selected bibliography that follows are those key books, articles, reports, and unpublished papers mentioned in the text.

In addition to the specific listings that follow, dozens of newsletters, journals, press releases, and magazines were consulted on a regular basis throughout the researching, and writing, of this book. Included in those categories are: *Marriage and Divorce Today, Monthly Vital Statistics, Commerce News, Solo, The Party Vine* newsletter, *Family Planning Perspectives, The Single Parent: Journal of Parents Without Partners, The Family Coordinator, Journal of Marriage and the Family, American Journal of Orthopsychiatry, Intercom, Adoption Report, Single Parent Family Project* newsletter, *SPFC Newsletter, Response to Violence and Sexual Abuse in the Family, National Council on Family Relations* newsletter, *Self-Help Reporter, American Journal of Psychiatry, American Sociological Review, U.S. News & World Report, Journal of the American Medical Association, Marriage & Family Review,* and others.

## BOOKS

Abeel, Erica. *Only When I Laugh.* New York: William Morrow, 1978.

Adams, Margaret. *Single Blessedness: Observations on the Single Status in Married Society.* New York: Penguin Books, 1978.

Ariès, Philippe. *Western Attitudes Toward Death from the Middle Ages to the Present.* Translated by Patricia M. Ranum. Baltimore, Md.: Johns Hopkins University Press, 1975.

Barkas, J. L. *The Help Book.* New York: Charles Scribner's Sons, 1979.

———. *Victims.* New York: Charles Scribner's Sons, 1978.

Bell, R. R. *Marriage and Family Interaction* 4th edition. Homewood, Ill.: Dorsey Press, 1975.

Bernard, Jessie. *The Future of Marriage.* New York: Bantam Books, 1973.

———. *Remarriage: A Study of Marriage.* New York: Russell & Russell, 1956, 1971.

Braudy, Susan. *Between Marriage and Divorce: A Woman's Diary.* New York: New American Library, 1975.

Caine, Lynn. *Widow.* New York: Bantam Books, 1975.

# BIBLIOGRAPHY

Carter, Hugh, and Glick, Paul C. *Marriage and Divorce: A Social and Economic Study*. Cambridge, Mass.: Harvard University Press, 1970.

Davis, Murray S. *Intimate Relations*. New York: Macmillan, The Free Press, 1973.

de Beauvoir, Simone. *The Second Sex*. Translated by H. M. Parshley. New York: Alfred A. Knopf, 1953.

Durkheim, Emile. *Suicide: A Study in Sociology*. Translated by John A. Spaulding and George Simpson. Edited by George Simpson. London: Routledge & Kegan Paul, 1897, 1952, 1970.

Edwards, Marie, and Hoover, Eleanor. *The Challenge of Being Single*. New York: New American Library, 1975.

Erikson, Erik H. *Childhood and Society* 2nd edition. New York: W. W. Norton, 1950, 1963.

Freedman, Jonathan. *Happy People: What Happiness Is, Who Has It, and Why*. New York: Harcourt Brace Jovanovich, 1978.

Freud, Anna. *The Ego and the Mechanisms of Defense* rev. ed. New York: International Universities Press, 1937, 1976.

Freud, Sigmund. *Civilization and Its Discontents*. Translated and edited by James Strachey. New York: W. W. Norton, 1961.

Friedan, Betty. *The Feminine Mystique*. New York: Dell Publishing Co., 1977.

Friedman, Bruce Jay. *The Lonely Guy's Book of Life*. New York: McGraw-Hill Book Co., 1978.

Fromm, Erich. *The Art of Loving*. New York: Harper & Row, 1956, 1974.

Gardner, Richard A. *The Boys and Girls Book About One-Parent Families*. New York: G. P. Putnam's Sons, 1978.

Gilder, George. *Naked Nomads*. New York: Quadrangle Books, 1974.

Gettleman, Susan, and Markowitz, Janet. *The Courage to Divorce*. New York: Simon & Schuster, 1974.

Godwin, John. *The Mating Trade*. Garden City, N.Y.: Doubleday, 1973.

Gordon, Barbara. *I'm Dancing As Fast As I Can*. New York: Harper & Row, 1979.

Gordon, Mary. *Final Payments*. New York: Ballantine Books, 1978.

Gordon, Suzanne. *Lonely in America*. New York: Simon & Schuster, Touchstone Books, 1976.

Greer, Germaine. *The Female Eunuch*. New York: Bantam Books, 1972.

Hite, Shere. *The Hite Report*. New York: Dell Publishing Co., 1976.

Hope, Karol, and Young, Nancy, eds. *MOMMA: The Sourcebook for Single Mothers*. New York: New American Library, 1976.

Howard, Jane. *Families*. New York: Simon & Schuster, 1978.

Hunt, Morton, and Hunt, Bernice. *The Divorce Experience*. New York: McGraw-Hill Book Co., 1977.

Johnson, Stephen M. *First Person Singular: Living the Good Life Alone*. Philadelphia: J. B. Lippincott, 1977.

Klein, Carole. *The Single Parent Experience*. New York: Avon Books, 1973.

Krantzler, Mel. *Creative Divorce*. New York: New American Library, 1973.

Kübler-Ross, Elisabeth. *On Death and Dying*. New York: Macmillan, 1969.

LeShan, Eda. *Learning to Say Good-by: When a Parent Dies*. New York: Macmillan, 1976.

Levin, Martin, ed. *Love Stories*. New York: Popular Library, 1975.

Lopata, Helena Znaniecka. *Women as Widows: Support Systems*. New York: Elsevier Nort Holland, 1979.

Lynch, James J. *The Broken Heart: The Medical Consequences of Loneliness*. New York: Basic Books, 1977, 1979.

Murstein, Bernard I., ed. *Exploring Intimate Life Styles*. New York: Springer Publishing Co., 1978.

Napolitane, Catherine, and Pellegrino, Victoria. *Living and Loving After Divorce*. New York: New American Library, 1978.

Parkes, Colin Murray. *Bereavement*. New York: International Universities Press, 1972.

Price, Richard. *Ladies' Man*. Boston: Houghton Mifflin, 1978.

Rogers, Carl R. *Becoming Partners: Marriage and Its Alternatives*. New York: Dell Publishing Co., 1972.

# BIBLIOGRAPHY

Shaine, Merle. *Some Men Are More Perfect Than Others.* New York: Bantam Books, 1974.

Sheehy, Gail. *Passages: Predictable Crises of Adult Life.* New York: Bantam Books, 1977.

Stein, Peter J. *Single.* Englewood Cliffs, N.J.: Prentice-Hall, 1976.

Szasz, Thomas. *The Second Sin.* Garden City, N.Y.: Doubleday, 1973.

Twain, Mark. *The Complete Short Stories of Mark Twain.* New York: Bantam Books, 1958.

Walster, Elaine, and Walster, G. William. *A New Look at Love.* Reading, Mass.: Addison-Wesley, 1978.

Weber, Eric. *How to Pick Up Girls.* New York: Symphony Press, 1970.

Weiss, Robert R. *Marital Separation.* New York: Basic Books, 1975.


## REPORTS, PAPERS, AND RELEASES

American Academy of Family Physicians. *A Report on Lifestyles/ Personal Health Care in Different Occupations: A Study of Attitudes and Practices.* Conducted by Research & Forecasts, a subsidiary of Ruder & Finn, Inc. Kansas City, Mo.: American Academy of Family Physicians, 1979.

Bachrach, Leona L. *Marital Status and Mental Disorder: An Analytical Review.* U.S. Department of Health, Education, and Welfare, Public Health Service, National Institute of Mental Health, Series D., No. 3. Washington, D.C.: U.S. Government Printing Office, 1975, 1978.

Bouvier, Leon F. "The Elderly Population: Its Relationship to Society." *Population Profiles,* 16. Washington, Conn.: Center for Information on America, 1976.

——, and Lee, Everett S. "The Bearing of Children." *Population Profiles,* 5. Washington, Conn.: Center for Information on America, 1975.

Espenshade, Thomas J. "The Value and Cost of Children." *Population Bulletin,* 32. Washington, D.C.: Population Reference Bureau, 1977.

Glick, Paul C., and Norton, Arthur J. "Marrying, Divorcing, and Living Together in the U.S. Today." *Population Bulletin,* 32. Washington, D.C.: Population Reference Bureau, 1977, updated reprint, 1979.

Levy, Richard A., Lt. Colonel, and Green, Jesse L., Major. "Time and Captivity: Prisoners of War in Vietnam and Since." Unpublished paper, 14-page typescript, 1978.

Masnick, George S., and McFalls, Joseph A., Jr. "Those Perplexing U.S. Fertility Swings: A New Perspective on a 20th Century Puzzle." *PRB Report.* Washington, D.C.: Population Reference Bureau, November 1978.

Masterson, James F., Jr. "Some Implications of the Sexual Revolution for Adolescents." Paper presented to a General Session of the American Medical Association, June 19, 1967, 15-page typescript.

Office of Population Censuses & Surveys, London. "Marriages, 1975 and 1976." Issued September 20, 1977.

Party Vine. *Directory of Selected Manhattan Singles Clubs.* New York: Party Vine, 1979.

*The Playboy Report on American Men: A Study of Values, Attitudes and Goals of U.S. Males 18-to-49 Years Old.* Poll conducted by Louis Harris and Associates, analysis and interpretation by William Simon, Ph.D., and Patricia Y. Miller, Ph.D. Chicago, Ill.: Playboy Enterprises, 1979.

Reilly, Mary Ellen. "The Family." *Population Profiles,* 17. Washington, Conn.: Center for Information on America, 1976.

"Research Shows Childfree Marriages Happiest." National Organization for Non-Parents (Maryland), January–February 1975 newsletter.

*Twenty Questions About Homosexuality: A Political Primer.* New York: Gay Activists Alliance, 1972.

U.S. Department of Commerce. "Census Bureau Projects Substantial Increase in Households by 1995." *Commerce News.* June 26, 1979 release. Washington, D.C.

————. "Less Change Ahead for American Family? Census Bureau Demographers Think So." *Commerce News.* February 15, 1979 release. Washington, D.C.

# BIBLIOGRAPHY

———. "Number of Single-Person Households Increases as Marriages Are Postponed, Census Bureau Reports." *Commerce News.* June 24, 1979 release. Washington, D.C.

———. "One Household in Five Consists of a Person Living Alone, Census Bureau Report Shows." *Commerce News.* March 17, 1976 release. Washington, D.C.

———. "Young, One-Person Households Increasing the Fastest, Census Bureau Reports." *Commerce News.* September 26, 1977 release. Washington, D.C.

U.S. Bureau of the Census, U.S. Department of Commerce. *Census of Population: 1970, Marital Status.* Final Report PC (2)-4C. Washington, D.C.: Government Printing Office, 1972.

———. *Current Population Reports,* Series P-20, No. 287. "Marital Status and Living Arrangements: March 1975." Washington, D.C.: U.S. Government Printing Office, 1976.

———. *Current Population Reports,* Series P-20, No. 323. "Marital Status and Living Arrangements: March 1977." Washington, D.C.: U.S. Government Printing Office, 1978.

———. *Current Population Reports,* Series P-20, No. 338. "Marital Status and Living Arrangements: March 1978." Washington, D.C.: U.S. Government Printing Office, 1979.

———. *Current Population Reports,* Series P-20, No. 349. "Household and Family Characteristics: March 1979." Washington, D.C.: U.S. Government Printing Office, 1980.

———. *We the American Women.* Washington, D.C.: U.S. Government Printing Office. No. 4 in series of reports from the 1970 Census.

———. *We, the American Young Marrieds.* Washington, D.C.: U.S. Government Printing Office, June 1973.

U.S. Department of Health, Education, and Welfare. *Facts About Mongolism for Women Over 35.* Washington, D.C.: U.S. Government Printing Office, 1973.

U.S. Department of Health, Education, and Welfare. National Center for Health Statistics. "Contraceptive Utilization Among Widowed, Divorced, and Separated Women in the United States: 1973 and 1976." *Advance Data,* September 22, 1978.

————. *Divorce and Divorce Rates: United States,* Series 21, No. 29. Washington, D.C.: U.S. Government Printing Office, March 1978.

————. "Teenage Childbearing: United States, 1966–75." *Monthly Vital Statistics Report,* September 8, 1977.

U.S. Department of Labor. "Single Men and Married Women Show Unusually Large Labor Force Gains." *News,* September 14, 1977 release. Washington, D.C.

*The 1980 Virginia Slims American Women's Opinion Poll.* Conducted by The Roper Organization, Inc., New York, 1980.

## JOURNAL, MAGAZINE, AND NEWSPAPER ARTICLES

Adams, Margaret. "The Single Woman in Today's Society: A Reappraisal." *American Journal of Orthopsychiatry* 41 (October 1971): 776–786.

American Family: "Not a Dying Institution." *USA Today* 107 (December 1978): 1–2.

Axelson, Leland J., and Glick, Paul C. "Family Specialists Look Ahead: Their Attitudes, Beliefs, Consensus, and Perceptions of Future Issues." *The Family Coordinator* 28 (April 1979): 149–155.

Barton, R. F. "Ifugao Law." *American Archaeology and Ethnology* 15 (February 15, 1919): 1–186.

"Being Single." *New York—WomensWeek,* July 17, 1978 issue.

Bell, Arthur. "Gay American Gothic: Norman in the Heartland?" *Village Voice,* May 21, 1979, pp. 1, 37–39.

Benson, Denzel E. "The Intentionally Childless Couple." *USA Today* 107 (January 1979): 45–46.

Bower, Donald W., and Christopherson, Victor A. "University Student Cohabitation: A Regional Comparison of Selected Attitudes and Behavior." *Journal of Marriage and the Family* 39 (August 1977): 447–452.

Brody, Jane E. "Marriage Is Good for Health and Longevity, Studies Say." *New York Times,* May 8, 1979, pp. C 1, 4.

# BIBLIOGRAPHY

Brozan, Nadine. "Women Who Waited: Starting a Family After the Age of 30." *New York Times,* September 23, 1977, p. B6.

Clayton, Richard R., and Voss, Harwin L. "Shacking Up: Cohabitation in the 1970's." *Journal of Marriage and the Family* 39 (May 1977): 273–283.

"Court Finds Out-of-Wedlock Life No Cause to Bar Virginia Lawyer." *New York Times,* April 21, 1979, p. 1.

Davidson, Joan K. "The Couple Assumption." *New York Times,* April 7, 1977, pp. Cl, 7.

Dullea, Georgia. "Artificial Insemination of Single Women Poses Difficult Questions." *New York Times,* March 9, 1979, p. A18.

"Easing the Plight of America's 1.8 Million Widowers." *U.S. News & World Report,* December 12, 1977, pp. 48–49.

Espenshade, Thomas J. "The Economic Consequences of Divorce." *Journal of Marriage and the Family* 41 (August 1979): 615–625.

Evans, Olive. "Married, Working, 30 Years Old—Is There Room for a Child?" *New York Times,* June 6, 1943, p. 42.

Francke, Linda Bird; Abramson, Pamela; Simons, Pamela Ellis; Copeland, Jeff; and Witman, Lisa. "Going It Alone." *Newsweek,* September 4, 1978, pp. 76–78.

Freud, Anna. "Adolescence." In *Psychoanalytic Study of the Child* 13 (1958): 255–278.

Glick, Paul C. "Social Change and the American Family." *Social Welfare Forum,* 1977, pp. 43–62.

Greenblat, Milton. "The Grieving Spouse." *American Journal of Psychiatry* 135 (January 1978): 43–47.

Gross, Amy. Marriage Counseling for Unwed Couples." *New York Times Magazine,* April 24, 1977, p. 52.

Hacker, Andrew. "Divorce à la Mode." *New York Review of Books,* May 3, 1979, pp. 23–27.

Herman, Robin. "Communal Life Adapts to Endure Decade of Change." *New York Times,* August 15, 1979, p. A20.

Hiltz, Starr Roxanne. "Widowhood: A Roleless Role." *Marriage & Family Review* 1 (November/December 1978): 1, 3–10.

Kaplan, Janice. "He/She." *Self,* March 1979, pp. 38, 40–41.

Kaplan, Samuel. "Single for Better or Worse." *Washington Post Book World,* June 4, 1978, pp. 1, 4.

Kidd, Virginia. "Happily Ever After." *Human Behavior,* June 1977, pp. 64–68.

Klemesrud, Judy. "Lesbians Who Try to Be Good Mothers." *New York Times,* January 31, 1973, p. 46.

Knupfer, Genevieve; Clark, Walter; and Room, Robin. "The Mental Health of the Unmarried." *American Journal of Psychiatry* (February 1966): 841–851.

Kyd, Joanna. "Unmarriage." *New York Times,* May 28, 1978, p. E15.

Lasswell, Marcia, and Lobsenz, Norman. "Love Vs. Privacy." *McCall's,* August 1977, pp. 46, 196.

Lazarre, Jane. "The High Cost of Living Off Someone Else." *Village Voice,* July 26, 1976, pp. 11–12.

Ledbetter, Les. "Jilted California Accountant Sues His Date for $38 in Expenses." *New York Times,* July 26, 1978, p. A10.

Lee, Gary R. "Age at Marriage and Marital Satisfaction: A Multivariate Analysis with Implications for Marital Stability." *Journal of Marriage and the Family* 39 (August 1977): 493–504.

Lindsey, Robert. "Lee Marvin Told to Pay $104,000, But Judge Prohibits Property Split." *New York Times,* April 19, 1979, pp. 1, B13.

"Loneliness: The New York Condition." *New York,* March 20, 1978, pp. 40–48.

Lovenheim, Barbara. "Singles: A Change of Scene." *New York Times,* March 15, 1978, p. C16.

Luepnitz, Deborah A. "Which Aspects of Divorce Affect Children?" *Family Coordinator* 28 (January 1979): 79–85.

McCarthy, James, and Menken, Jane. "Marriage, Remarriage, Marital Disruption and Age at First Birth." *Family Planning Perspectives* 11 (January/February 1979): 21–30.

McMahon, Judi. "Sensational Female Seeks Male Equal for Serious Sharing." *New York,* April 2, 1979, pp. 59–62.

"Manhattan Singles," August 17, 1979 issue of *Cue.*

"Marriage and Divorce." *Harper's Weekly,* March 28, 1979, pp. 1, 8–9.

Mead, Margaret. "Apprenticeship for Marriage: A Startling Proposal." *Redbook*, October 1963, pp. 14, 16.

———. "A Continuing Dialogue on Marriage: Why Just 'Living Together' Won't Work." *Redbook*, April 1968, pp. 44, 46, 48, 50–51, 119.

———. "Marriage in Two Steps." *Redbook*, July 1966, pp. 48–49, 81, 86.

"Men Write to Challenge Single Women's Criticism." *New York Times*, August 5, 1978, p. 12.

Nemy, Enid. "The Urban Widow: 'I Realized I Didn't Want to Marry Again.'" *New York Times*, March 16, 1979, p. A20.

Neubeck, Gerhard. "In Praise of Marriage." *Family Coordinator* 28 (January 1979): 115–117.

Newcomb, Paul R. "Cohabitation in America: An Assessment of Consequences." *Journal of Marriage and the Family* 41 (August 1979): 597–603.

New York Telephone Company. "How to live alone in New York without feeling lonely." Advertisement in *New York Times*, April 16, 1979, p. B12.

Nobile, Philip. "The Meaning of Gay" (an interview with Dr. C. A. Tripp). *New York*, June 25, 1979, pp. 36–41.

"Of Women, Knights and Horses." *Time*, January 1, 1979, p. 64.

Olds, Sally Wendkos. "How to Stay Close in Love Without Losing Your Self." *Redbook*, April 1978, pp. 107, 164, 166, 168.

Pearlin, Leonard I., and Johnson, Joyce S. "Marital Status, Life-Strains, and Depression." *American Sociological Review* 42 (October 1977): 704–715.

Phillips, Melanie. "Bachelors Replace Spinsters." (Manchester) *Guardian*, April 8, 1979, p. 5.

Reinhold, Robert. "Trend to Living Alone Brings Economic and Social Change." *New York Times*, March 20, 1977, pp. 1, 59.

Robertson, Nan. "Single Women Over 30: 'Where Are the Men Worthy of Us?'" *New York Times*, July 14, 1978, p. A12.

Sauer, Raymond J. "Absentee Father Syndrome." *Family Coordinator* 28 (April 1979): 245–249.

Schmeck, Harold M., Jr. "Amniocentesis in Pregnancy Safe, Study Indicates." *New York Times*, October 21, 1975, p. 46.

Schorr, Alvin L., and Moen, Phyllis. "The Single Parent and Public Policy." *Social Policy* 9 (March/April 1979): 15–21.

Snyder, Alice Ivey. "Periodic Marital Separation and Physical Illness." *American Journal of Orthopsychiatry* 48 (October 1978): 637–643.

Solocheck, Beverly. "Unmarried Couples Look for Equity in Co-ops." *New York Times,* September 4, 1977, pp. 1, 3, sect. 8.

Somers, Anne R. "Marital Status, Health, and Use of Health Services: An Old Relationship Revisited." *Journal of American Medical Association* 241 (April 27, 1979): 1818–1822.

Spreitzer, Elmer, and Riley, Lawrence E. "Factors Associated with Singlehood." *Journal of Marriage and the Family* (August 1974): 533–542.

Stein, Peter J. "The Lifestyles and Life Chances of the Never-Married: A Review of the Recent Literature." *Marriage & Family Review* 1 (July/August 1978): 1, 3–10.

"Unmarried Life Style." June 10–23, 1978 issue of *Cue.*

"U.S. Women Marrying Later, Having Babies Later, Spacing Them Further Apart Than in Earlier Years." *Family Planning Perspectives* 10 (September/October 1978): 302.

van Gelder, Lawrence. "Lawyers Troubled by Rehabilitation Concept in Marvin Decision." *New York Times,* April 20, 1979, p. A18.

Wolfe, Linda. "Why Some People Can't Love" (an interview with Otto Kernberg). *Psychology Today,* June 1978, pp. 55–59.

Younger, Judith T. "Reflections on Marriage Law: Its Revision and Reformation." *Cornell Law Forum* 6 (June 1979): 8–11.

Yurasits, Victoria. "Does Separation Have to Mean Divorce?" *Redbook,* January 1977, pp. 93, 131, 133.

Zabin, Laurie Schwab; Kantner, John F.; and Zelnik, Melvin. "The Risk of Adolescent Pregnancy in the First Months of Intercourse." *Family Planning Perspectives* 11 (July/August 1979): 215, 217–222.

J. L. Barkas has taught at Temple University and The New School for Social Research. Her articles, essays, and reviews have appeared in dozens of publications, including *The New York Times, Harper's, McCall's, Glamour, Redbook, Family Circle,* and *The New Leader.* Barkas is the author of several books, including *Victims* and *The Help Book.*